Hey BOBBY
YOU GUYS HAVE
A GREAT TEAM.
THOROUGHLY ENJOYED
THE INTERVIEW

ADAM
x

SMALL CHANGE BIG DIFFERENCE

THE PENNY APPEAL STORY

TSB

ADEEM YOUNIS

SMALL CHANGE BIG DIFFERENCE

THE PENNY APPEAL STORY

TSB
London and New York

Small Change, BIG DIFFERENCE
The Penny Appeal Story

9 8 7 6 5 4 3 2 1

First published by TSB, 2021
TSB is an imprint of:
Can of Worms Enterprises Ltd
7 Peacock Yard
London SE17 3LH
United Kingdom
www.canofworms.net

Cover design: Convey
Typesetting: James Shannon

Printed and bound in the United Kingdom by
TJ Books Ltd, Padstow, Cornwall

ISBN: 978-1-911673-10-1 (hardback)
ISBN: 978-1-911673-11-8 (paperback)
ISBN: 978-1-911673-12-5 (ebook)

British Library Cataloguing in Publication Data
A catalogue record for this book is available from the British Library

Penny Appeal is a UK registered charity 1128341

To Mum, for your unwavering love, support, mentoring and inspiration over the last forty years. Without you, I wouldn't be in the position to tell the story of Penny Appeal – because without your influence, it wouldn't exist.

To Hajrah, Aayisha, Abdullah and Ruquiyah. The world is a better place for having each of you. You will forever be my inspiration; I love you all more than anything.

CONTENTS

PREFACE

James Caan, "I'm in!" Penny Appeal meeting in Wakefield

"BUT THERE WAS SOMETHING UNUSUAL ABOUT THIS YOUNG MAN SAT NEXT TO ME, AND WHEN HE TOLD ME THAT IN EIGHT YEARS HE'D GROWN A CHARITY CALLED PENNY APPEAL INTO A £20 MILLION-A-YEAR FOUNDATION, I PAID ATTENTION."

I first met Adeem Younis in 2017, at a charity dinner in London. I have many interests and responsibilities in the charity world, and I often meet good-hearted people who, in their own ways, are doing something to improve the world. But there was something unusual about this young man sat next to me, and when he told me that in eight years he'd grown a charity called Penny Appeal into a £20 million-a-year foundation, I paid attention. I know from experience that when you raise that kind of money, you can really begin to make a difference.

Three years on, I'm now happy to be known as an ambassador for my friend Adeem's amazing charity, which I've witnessed bring about lasting change for countless individuals and families.

JAMES CAAN

I've visited the sites of Penny Appeal's incredible programmes, which are breaking the cycle of poverty at every point: supporting orphans, building clean wells, fixing eyesight, feeding the poor and needy, turning up at short notice to deliver vital aid at crisis hotspots. Nor has the growth stopped: in 2019, Penny Appeal topped £30 million in charitable donations. Over the past ten years, it has raised over £100 million.

This book tells the story of the first ten years of Penny Appeal's remarkable life. I'm proud to have played a small part in its history, and I'm certainly in for the next stage of its development, as it continues to grow and deliver vital programmes in Asia, the Middle East, Africa and the UK.

James Caan CBE, London

CHAPTER ONE

CROSSROADS

Adeem and Dr Bilal on pilgrimage to Makkah, 2018

I made my fifth pilgrimage to Makkah at the end of December 2018. I have been fortunate to be able to make these trips: there are millions of Muslims all over the world who long to make the pilgrimage, but who will never have the funds to be able to do so. This was my first visit in ten years, and I had particular reasons for wanting to complete the sacred ritual of Umrah, the lesser pilgrimage in the Islamic tradition. Often, I disappear on holiday during the Christmas season, but that year I felt a strong need to make the Umrah.

I travelled to Saudi Arabia with my long-standing Penny Appeal colleague and friend, Dr Bilal, and we met up with a group from the US that included Sheikh Hisham Mahmoud, an esteemed scholar of Islam. The first element of Umrah was to wear *ihram* clothing, which for men consists of two plain white sheets of unstitched cloth. *Ihram* levels you, strips back all the layers of who you think you are. Prince or pauper, you wear the same two white sheets. We're all equal before God.

The second rite of the Umrah is the Tawaf, the sevenfold walk around the Kaaba – the immense black building at the heart of the sacred Great Mosque – all the while reciting various prayers and supplications. Dr Bilal is a mountain of a man, and I was clinging onto his arm as we circled the building amidst hundreds of thousands of pilgrims that New Year's Eve. As we walked, according to instruction, I prayed for those I did not know, and for those I did: my family, friends and colleagues. Eventually, I turned my prayers to myself. I knew I was seeking guidance; I knew there was a reason I had wanted to complete Umrah that year.

I was thirty-eight years old. Twenty years earlier, while still a teenager, I had started my first Internet business above a pizza shop in Wakefield, Northern England. Within a few years, the Muslim-marriage introduction agency I founded, Single Muslim, had made me a wealthy man. Now we were a global marriage-introduction brand, probably the biggest in the world, with three million members. I had won my freedom through an intense work ethic, an entrepreneur's instinct for picking the right people along the way, an optimist's willingness to champion talent. I was a successful business owner, but I knew my business could do more.

Once I had begun to accrue some capital from Single Muslim, and while still a young man, I became increasingly motivated by the desire to support those less fortunate than I in my family's homeland in Gujar Khan, north-eastern Pakistan. Charity in Islam is considered to be an act of worship, and is an obligation placed upon all believers. As my earnings grew from my entrepreneurial activities, I found myself spending more and more time looking to make my own charitable giving as effective as I could. As I learned more about what my family's ancestral home in the Gujar Khan region needed, I began to understand that the cycles of poverty I had witnessed there were repeated all over the world. Eventually, it just seemed logical to create a charitable organisation. In 2009, I founded Penny Appeal and became one of its first three trustees.

In ten years, Penny Appeal had raised over £100 million, and had delivered food and aid to needy people in over fifty countries. We'd never been a conventional charity. From Day One, we used my entrepreneurial instinct – and the commercial marketing techniques I'd sweated for years at Single Muslim to perfect – to create the most efficient machine possible for honouring the charitable obligations of Islam. We were digitally savvy, and early adopters of online fundraising; we staged record-breaking TV fundraising marathons; toured films, music and stand-up comedy around the UK as a way of getting face-to-face with our Muslim donors and requesting their donations; generated hundreds of local jobs, including a huge telephone sales operation covering massive office

SingleMuslim.com success story, Alam and Safiyyah with Adeem, 2007

floorspace. We never followed any charity formula: we deployed marketing and communication skills to reach out to young millennials who used cutting-edge social media, as well as older and wealthier donors. We did all this so that we could deliver as much charitable work as possible.

By the time I found myself praying that New Year's Eve in Makkah, Penny Appeal's Feed Our World programme had delivered a staggering 7.5 million meals to beneficiaries around the globe. We had provided aid to over 1.7 million people suffering after unexpected tragedies, from the earthquake in

Haiti to the terrible fire at Grenfell Tower in London. We had put over 50,000 orphan children through education, given care sponsorships to 7,000 elderly people and ensured the supply of 3 billion glasses of clean water to people living in rural poverty around the world. In ten years, we had become one of the most significant Muslim charities in the UK, and had completely changed the way British Muslims thought about charitable giving.

We always wanted to be bigger and better, so that we could help as many people as possible. That was what drove us, obsessed us. In the ten years leading up to the formation of Penny Appeal in 2009, I had worked night and day to build Single Muslim into the world's most successful online marriage agency, and in doing so I had learned from hard, tough experience how to operate more effectively than anyone else in the online world. I'd brought those skills into the new charity, ruffling more than a few feathers by using my hard-earned commercial knowledge to develop better ways of communicating with Muslim donors than all the charities that had gone before me. I used my commercial income to incubate Penny Appeal, to give it the breathing space it needed to grow. None of it had been easy. For a kid from a very poor family in Wakefield, I'd had to fight for every inch of success I achieved. That made me passionately protective of the charity I'd founded, and determined to see it continue growing, so that it could reach more and more needy people everywhere.

Now, as I trembled in prayer, I asked God to guide me through the next steps I had to take. I needed clarity on a crucial question: did Penny Appeal need me anymore? After ten years, we had a staff of over 100, working under a chief executive I'd appointed four years earlier. It was a slick, professional charity that, with every passing year, raised more money and helped more people. I had passed on all I had learned about online

"We always wanted to be bigger and better, so that we could help as many people as possible. That was what drove us, obsessed us."

marketing, TV advertising, staging live events, maintaining the loyalty of donors through smart communication. I had personally supported the charity financially for years, but now it was quite capable of standing on its own two feet.

Was it time now for me to step back, focus once more on my private business and let my many gifted, talented and incredibly hard-working colleagues take the charity forward into a new era of success and expansion? I had never taken a salary from Penny Appeal, and had worked as an unpaid trustee for ten years; maybe the time was right for me to plunge fully back into my commercial business. I'm an entrepreneur; I'm a very demanding person to work for. I've overcome a lot of very big challenges in my life, and I probably don't realise how much I expect of other people. So should I let others now steer the charity into the future? Had I done all I could do?

I'm not a man to wear his heart on his sleeve. Until recently, I presented quite an enigmatic face to the people around me, never really letting anyone in close enough to find out what I was thinking. As much as I inspired people to achieve the best of which they were capable, I also mystified them. *What makes Adeem tick?* I knew that question was on many people's lips, but I never gave anyone the satisfaction of knowing the answer. *That's just how God made me,* is what I thought. And now, deep in prayer that night in Makkah, I sought His guidance. I couldn't turn to anyone I knew for advice; that wasn't how I conducted myself. But I needed to know how to move forward. I sought help.

We walked around and around the Kaaba. It's said that we move counterclockwise, mimicking angels doing the same overhead, so that our hearts incline towards the centre, yearning to return to their Creator. I looked up towards the clock face that towers over the Great Mosque like an exaggerated version of London's Big Ben. The minute hand was just closing on the twelve. The year 2018 came to an end that very moment, and we entered 2019. In every other major city of the world, that moment would have sparked a cacophony of celebrations and fireworks, but this was not like any other city. The mesmerising buzz of pilgrims continued from one moment to the next, each of us immersed in our worship, some crying, some smiling, some being pushed in wheelchairs and others almost jogging. Every type of human being was present: old, young, black, brown, white and every shade in between. All were focused on God; nothing else was important. I turned to Dr Bilal and wished him Happy New Year. Around us, other pilgrims began to do the same. It was a moment I shall never forget.

The following day, after we had undergone the traditional blade shave of our hair, which symbolises renewal, we spent several hours with Sheikh Mahmoud in our hotel room close by. He spoke to us with great wisdom and authority about the history of the Great Mosque, the people who built it and the truths it represented. As he explained to us with such eloquence and knowledge, I reflected on the people he was describing from over 1,400 years ago, and began to understand the significance of their legacy. As I did that, I wondered: what legacy shall we leave? What will we be able to point to at the righteous hour and say: *This is what I did?*

I had reached a crossroads, and didn't know which way to turn. I felt powerless in the face of the decisions I was grappling with. But God is the greatest of planners. All we need to do is to accept His will. I received an answer to my prayer that very same year in an entirely unexpected, absolutely shocking way, just months after we all walked slowly, patiently and humbly around the Kaaba. I hope you don't mind if I tell you the story.

"Now, as I trembled in prayer, I asked God to guide me through the next steps I had to take. I needed clarity on a crucial question: did Penny Appeal need me anymore?"

CHAPTER TWO

WAKEFIELD, CENTRE OF THE UNIVERSE

Penny Appeal was born inside the mind of a child on a street in Wakefield, Northern England, in 1988.

I'm six years old and I've spent the last few weeks visiting my dad in hospital, in his bed surrounded by flowers, religious elders, bottles of the blessed Zamzam water from Makkah, the heavy smell of attar. I'm not really sure what's wrong with Dad, but each time I visit him I pick some daffodils from our front garden; Mum will take them from me and put them in another vase beside his bed.

Dad's from the same Gujar Khan area in north-eastern Pakistan as Mum's family – the same region from which more than half of all British Pakistanis originated. Dad came from a tiny village called Roohan, even now an hour's uncomfortable car journey from Mum's village, Hathia Dhamial. They were teenagers when they married in 1979; now Dad's just thirty-two years old, and he's been lying in this hospital bed in Wakefield for what seems like forever to me.

Pakistanis from Gujar Khan started settling in Britain in the 1940s, transferring their workmanship on British merchant navy ships to the industrial needs of the growing British economy. The mill chimneys of the industrial North attracted immigrant workers from a largely rural region of Pakistan, where there was little experience of urban living. These enterprising people brought traditional Muslim values of hard work, family life, respect for faith and determination to prosper. They left behind a land of arid and uneven pastures, where education was often unknown, and life was harsh. When the government of the young Islamic Republic of Pakistan decided to construct the huge Mangla Dam in 1966, vast areas of farmland in the district were submerged, and over 110,000 people were displaced. Many were given work permits for Britain; the booming '60s British economy was short on workers to fuel its hunger.

Mum and Dad were firmly part of this Pakistani diaspora,

relocated from the high, barren plateaus and deep, narrow valleys of the land bordering Kashmir and the Himalayas to the puffing chimneys and winding streets of the industrial North of England. Families from my parents' region settled in and around Bradford, Wakefield and, 100 miles down south, Birmingham and the Black Country. They had family in the same street, and cousins not far away in Bradford and Manchester, and continued the daily pattern of life in Pakistan, rising early, working all hours, attending prayers at the mosque. The community was tightly knit, separated from their new fellow citizens by their brown skin and, often, their lack of English. The men tended to be more gregarious, working alongside white men at the mill and in the factories, although that gregariousness ended when their English colleagues piled into the pubs and clubs after work; my dad and the other teetotal Pakistanis headed home to family. The women remained indoors much of the time, cooking and looking after children, sometimes never learning the difficult new language at all.

Why's Dad in hospital?

My dad is tall and good-looking; he's the centre of the community in our street in Wakefield. He works at the mill less than half a mile from our house, and has passed the exams to get his taxi badge. He's got Mum and me and my two younger sisters. We've got my uncle, Mum's brother, in the house next door, and another uncle three doors down.

What's he doing in that bed? Why isn't he at home with me and the family, like all the other dads?

Now I'm walking up our street. Suddenly there are cars parked everywhere, and the front garden is filled with shoes. When I go in the house there's a coffin in the hallway and all you can hear are Asian women wailing. Everyone's hugging me and kissing me, and I find myself stuck in this crowd of people. Then one of my aunties looks at me and starts screaming. She

"At that moment, I decide that the little boy who is the centre of all that hysterical attention isn't me."

looks up at the ceiling and wails:

"What have you done, God! What have you done! Why have you done this, why have you done this!" She grabs hold of me. "What is he going to do? Tell me, God, what is he going to do? What's going to happen to him now?"

I am gathered up by someone else, but still my auntie is screaming: "You've taken him away, you've taken him away .... They've got nothing now, they've got nothing .... What will happen to the boy?"

The only thing I can think of doing is to pretend that this isn't happening. *What does she mean, what am I going to do? Have I done something wrong? What does Auntie mean, what's going to happen to me? I don't want anything to happen to me.*

At that moment, I decide that the little boy who is the centre of all that hysterical attention isn't me. My dad hasn't died of cancer. I live in Wakefield, knock conkers off the tree with my friend Billy, chase pretty Karen around the schoolyard. I put the memory of that day away in a box. I lock it and throw the key over my shoulder.

A couple of months later, I'm in a classroom surrounded by boys, and they're laughing. One of them is reading out the surnames from the class register on the teacher's desk. He goes through them, one at a time. Then when he gets to mine, he shouts:

"'Deceased'! Adeem's dad's name is 'Deceased'!"

Adeem with his dad, aged 5

The school had written the word next to my dad's name in the register.

Then the teacher comes in, tells everyone to sit down and says, "Class, you need to understand that Adeem's father is deceased, meaning that he's dead."

I'm thinking, *no he's not, my dad's not dead.* I say it out loud: "Guys, you got it wrong. My dad's not dead. My dad's not dead."

○

And so the front door to our house in Wakefield, where my mum still lives, became a border. Once I'd crossed that border, I was back home with my family, with the knowledge that Dad had died, having to get used to uncles and aunties visiting, placing their hands on my head in pity, slipping a coin in my pocket, leaving me a hand-me-down toy they'd brought from their own homes.

On the other side of the front door was a world where no one had to know that I didn't have a dad, where I didn't have to fear what might happen to me because I'd lost one of my parents. I kept strict control of that border, never letting my white friends in: they would never know my secret. I policed my own childhood and kept my vigilance going for at least another twenty-five years.

Soon after Dad's passing, my *babaji* (grandfather), my mum's dad, came to live with us. Grandad was a veteran of the British Army, a man with huge generosity of spirit, rigid discipline and endless compassion and wisdom. I had my own bed in the corner of the room we shared, and every morning he would look over to check that I had made my bed, cleaned my shoes, ironed my shirt. Grandad prayed five times a day; nothing would get in the way of his daily prayers. He smoked for Britain, but that was before he moved in with us. Nowadays the only thing he smoked was the nebuliser face mask he had to wear four times a day to help him breathe.

He was a philosophical man, full of practical wisdom. Once I asked him why some members of our family didn't talk to others. He said: "Adeem, we are all children of Adam and Eve; in some ways, we are all family. So if we all had to go to each other's houses for birthdays and celebrations, imagine what it would be like; we would all have to talk to everyone … we'd never get anything done." That made perfect sense to me.

Grandad became a source of comfort and security. Even in my twenties, as I began to build my own business, I would come back and sit beside him, telling him what I was doing. He would try and make sense of it all, nod his head thoughtfully, put his hand on my arm. I knew he couldn't really understand the new digital age I was telling him about, but it was crucial that he was there for me to tell him anyway.

Of course, the most important influence in my life – then as now – was Mum. She had three children to support single-handedly, and wasn't even thirty-five years old. When she left Pakistan at the age of nineteen, she couldn't read or write English. To this day, I am still humbled by what she achieved, how she looked after my two sisters and me, sustained our family within the community in Wakefield, taught us how to conduct ourselves. She is the most remarkable person I have ever known.

Early on, Mum began taking in sewing, doing piecework for garment manufacturers in town. Regularly, there would be piles of clothing in our house; we all learned how to sew buttons, insert zips, attach pockets to the backs of jeans. With piecework, faulty workmanship didn't get paid, so we kids had it drilled in us that we needed to be careful and diligent to ensure that all the clothes were accepted by the supplier for the rate of 2p per piece. Before long, Mum opened up her

Adeem with his grandad, aged 13

own market stall, selling her own products. Later, she had the incredible bravery to open up her own shop just off Brook Street, in the centre of Wakefield.

I've since discovered how much of a role model Mum became for Asian women in Wakefield, how they watched and learned from this young widow with three children, who never thought twice about seizing every opportunity to provide for her family. Although it wasn't considered becoming in the community for women to do so, she even learned how to drive, and scraped together the money to buy a beat-up old Nissan Micra that she used to drive us to school and take us to our extracurricular activities.

I knew even then how unusual it was for a mum to be doing all the things she did, but that didn't stop me from asking her to drop me round the corner from school every morning, so that my friends wouldn't see my mother behind the wheel of an old Micra. I didn't want anyone to know a thing about our family; I wouldn't let the outside world peep through the crack of our front door. In retrospect, of course, everyone *did* know. Mum couldn't afford to buy new school clothes for us, so we used to go to the Yorkshire Purchasing Organisation, which gave them to low-income families for free. They were the lowest-budget clothes you could get: squeaky plastic raincoats, rough hairy socks. You could tell a "YPO kid" a mile off.

The terrible drama of that day at our house in 1987 also made me realise that I would have to earn money. I couldn't let Mum take on all the burden, and Grandad was too old and weakened by the cigarettes that would eventually kill him. From the age of eight, I was thus always on the lookout for ways to make money, which I'd bring home to Mum for her to allocate. At school, the poor kids used to get free meal vouchers. You were made to stand over to one side from the other students while you waited for your food: you were in the queue of poor kids,

"Those pennies I'd earn as a cheeky ten-year-old, pinching discarded tennis rackets out of skips, would return almost twenty years later in the very name and concept of Penny Appeal."

kids who didn't have a dad. The tokens were worth £1.50, so I used to sell mine to other greedy kids for a discounted price of 90p, and spend some of that on a smaller lunch. That way I got the double benefit of bringing home a bit of cash for Mum, and also avoided being paraded in front of all the others as a poor, fatherless child.

There were countless ways you could make a few pennies in Wakefield back then. My mate Billy and I discovered that the local Slazenger factory would chuck away tennis rackets that had developed faults during manufacture. We saw them sticking out of big skips. One night we climbed into a skip the size of a house to grab as many as we could hold with our skinny arms. Then we took them down to the market and offered them to traders, who were happy to have some budget items to offload.

I did paper rounds, stacked shelves at the local corner shop, manned market stalls, delivered milk early in the morning; I did anything I could to bring money into the house. Although I was just a child, I knew it was my responsibility. Mum never once made me feel like I had to do that; it was all of my own doing.

Even so, she welcomed the extra income.

As I write this, I realise how far back the seeds of Penny Appeal go. The trauma of my dad's passing, combined with my determination not to reveal it or its impact to the world outside our front door, stayed with me for many, many years. Only recently have I been able to speak of it. But it worked away inside me, so that when I reached the age of eighteen and began making trips on my own to our family's village in north-eastern Pakistan, I found myself involved in the stories of the village orphans, found it impossible *not* to want to do something to help them. Yet even as I began to explore what I might be able to do, I still didn't admit the motivation to myself.

And those pennies I'd earn as a cheeky ten-year-old, pinching discarded tennis rackets out of skips, would return almost twenty years later in the very name and concept of Penny Appeal. I handed over every penny I made to Mum, who used them to increase the safety and security of our family. Small change, big difference.

○

Wakefield in the late 1980s and early 1990s was a different place than it is now. Let me describe a scene to you:

I was maybe twelve years old. I'd left school early, as I wasn't feeling well. It was a sunny day and I suddenly felt sick, so I hopped up on a wall to take a breath. The wall bordered the front garden of a terraced house. As soon as I'd sat down, I heard a little girl's voice call out behind me:

"Mummy! Mummy! There's a Paki sitting on our wall!"

I turned around and saw a little white girl, no more than five years old, staring at me from the open window of a ground-floor room.

And I actually looked around, wondering where this "Paki"

she was talking about was sitting.

Then it struck home. She was talking about me.

Racism was endemic in Wakefield when I was growing up. There were certain streets you didn't walk down, for fear of being spat at or attacked. You'd be careful walking past the Working Men's Club a few hundred yards from our house when last orders had been called, because the middle-aged white men spilling out into the street would often launch into a terrifying volley of verbal abuse as soon as they caught sight of you. I took karate lessons at the martial arts place near our home, and soon learned to defend myself. I learned how to look after myself – skinny little Paki though I was.

The sense of being "other" manifested itself in so many ways. One Saturday night, after I'd left school for college, I discovered that some students I believed were my close friends were all going to a barbecue. Everyone but me had been invited. I asked one of my friends why.

"We didn't think you'd enjoy it, Adeem. We know, you guys don't drink, do you?"

I resisted that ghetto mentality. Despite everything, I went through my childhood genuinely feeling that I could be friends with anyone. I didn't see it as making a point; I just like people, and enjoy meeting them. I've always been like that: no one was ever too poor or too rich for me to speak to. If I could have a hot dinner for every time I've been described as "naive", I'd be a lot tubbier than I am now. But that naivety, if that's what it is, somehow insulated me from the racism that ran so deep in Northern industrial towns. When it did make some kind of impact on me, I was always surprised, because Wakefield was and still is my home. I'm a Northerner; I speak like a Northerner, I think like a Northerner, I drink flipping *tea* like a Northerner. I could have left Wakefield years ago, moved to London, emigrated to Silicon Valley to seek my fortune. But then I'd have become rootless, adrift. Life only really makes sense to me if I know I've still just got time to get to the Tesco in Stanley Road to buy some full-fat milk on the way home after another day at work.

So I grew up with racism. Yet I refused to let it either identify me, or scar me. That's been another of the fundamental principles of Penny Appeal: we're a British Muslim charity, and to my mind, both words have equal weight. I'm proud of my country, proud of being British, of being a Yorkshireman. Early on in our history, we introduced the notion that for every pound we spend abroad, we'll spend a pound at home. We still strive for that. When floods devastated Cumbria in 2015, Penny Appeal was one of the first organisations on the scene. In 2017, our people were at the dreadful Grenfell Tower fire within hours. Our Team Orange volunteers provide food to homeless people all over Britain, and we have specially trained practitioners on hand seven days a week to listen to and guide people who are suffering from domestic abuse.

I don't want it to seem unusual that a Muslim charity should allocate so much of its donation to non-Muslim recipients here at home. To me, that's just what communities do: we look after each other. And we British *are* a community, no matter how much politics may divide us. The racism of my childhood in Wakefield is no longer the obvious and frequently violent problem it once was. It hasn't disappeared, but we're removing the barriers that alienate us – and I'm proud to be part of that change.

Faith was always an important part of our household. As I've said, Grandad prayed five times daily. He was often too poorly to make it to the mosque, but would encourage me to do so. Everyone in our family – all our uncles and aunties in the street – would attend prayers at the mosque. As a religion, a guiding force, Islam has always made sense to me. I have never had moments of doubt that its teaching provides a practical framework for life. Love your neighbour; help those who are less fortunate than you; give a little, but give regularly; even a smile is charity.

At the same time, growing up in the circumstances I did, I often found myself questioning some interpretations of the faith by elders at the mosque. I remember being told: *Adeem, a true Muslim will always read the Qur'an in Arabic.* But I'm English, I'd say. I won't understand it if I read it in Arabic. If I read the Qur'an in translation, I'll understand it, and I'll be able to implement its teachings more effectively. The men at our mosque were mainly taxi drivers or factory workers, the majority of them from the Mirpur region of Pakistan. Doesn't Allah appeal to others, I'd ask? Where are all the other Muslims? Mum saved up enough money to send me on my first Umrah when I reached eighteen. In Makkah, I was amazed to find myself amongst Chinese people, black people, white people – all of them Muslims, all making the pilgrimage together, sharing and caring in a beautiful, peaceful way of true sincerity and brotherhood. When I got back to Wakefield, I found another mosque in the city attended by women, blacks, whites, Egyptians, Somalis. This environment seemed more natural to me, and I started going to that mosque while Mum, Grandad and the rest of the family continued to go to the other. Even today, in Wakefield, someone will come up to me and say, *Adeem, you should grow your beard longer; you should wear a cap in the mosque.* I'm forty years old, and someone's telling me to grow my beard longer!

But I understand, now that I'm a little older, how life and faith can be difficult things to balance, particularly when you are struggling to keep afloat. One day I was late home from school, having decided to save bus fare by walking. As I passed through the centre of the city, a girl from my class waved at me, and we walked for five minutes chatting until she headed off in her direction and I continued on my way back home. During that same space of time, someone from my community spotted *Adeem Younis with a girl!* and reported the fact back to Mum. When I returned home, she asked me why I was so late. I told her I'd decided to save the fare, and she gave me an almighty slap on the face and repeated the question. When I gave the same answer, she hit me again. She accused me of deliberately meeting up with girls and bringing shame upon the family. She hit me once more and sent me to bed. Later that evening, she brought me some food and apologised. "Sometimes," she said, "it all gets too much for me ... but I always want the best for you, and I don't ever want anyone to say that you weren't raised properly because you didn't have a father."

Growing up as a Muslim in the North of England can be confusing. Faith is the anchor that holds you fast, but that doesn't mean you don't face doubt and confusion in your daily life. It's the same for everyone. I asked controversial questions, but that's just part of being alive. I don't even consider myself to be especially non-traditional; when I visit our Muslim colleagues in the US, Canada and Australia these days, their liberal approach to our faith can often make me feel like the elders at our mosque in Wakefield must have felt when I challenged them!

I had one other secret, though, one further layer of insecurity that I'd kept hidden from the world, even from my family. Since that day when all the cars were parked in our street and I saw the shoes scattered in our front garden, I knew I wouldn't have long here. Dad was thirty-three when he died, so it was obvious to me: I only had another twenty-five years or so left. It was inevitable; there was no point talking about it – what good would that do? That was simply the allocation God had given Dad and me. He had His reasons, and I accepted that. I would die young, and the friends I was growing up with would live on for decades, seeing children and grandchildren. Not me.

Thirty years later, I find that I'm still here. I have four beautiful children, one more than my dad. I have a successful business, and lead a fantastic global charity. I've finally had to accept that I have been wrong about the assumption I made when Dad left us. The only guarantee is that death *will* come and collect us all one day; early or late, we all have to go. Dad might have passed on his curly hair to me, but I'm starting to understand now that I didn't need to lock that secret into my heart as a six-year-old boy. Maybe I won't ever really stop believing it, but at least now I can see the possibility of a future. For most of my life, I never thought I had one.

When you think like that, when you have such a secret inner conviction, it makes you *impatient* – not like when you ask the old fellow in front of you at the post office to hurry up, but in the sense of feeling that things need to be achieved as quickly as possible. There is no time to waste: results must be found, whatever it takes. With this mindset, certainty takes hold that if something is wrong, it needs to be fixed, changed, improved, right *now*. Not "later", not next week. Now.

I'm twenty-one. One thing that annoys me about the mosque is that there's no library. Reading is really important to me, and when we young people go to the mosque, there's nothing to do there. You put your shoes in a horrible old rack; the carpet's sticky; the toilets are smelly, with smelly towels. It's a cold space, unappealing, and certainly not motivating in any way. You go in, sit, recite a foreign language; then you go home again. The non-Muslim world out there competes for your attention with nightclubs, casinos, entertainment complexes. And so I think: why can't there be more to do at the mosque?

I make a full-blown presentation to the committee, explaining why they need to have a library there, and a computer, too, so that kids can interact more, watch videos, surf the Internet, learn about stuff. They resist, telling me that a good Muslim doesn't worry about external stuff like this; *good Muslims just have faith.*

But for me, faith comes precisely from being inspired, seeing what you want to be, all whilst believing in the power of the Unseen because it *grips* you. Faith comes from the experience of every aspect of our surroundings, but I was losing faith on account of the experience I had at the mosque.

With such conviction, I persuade them, and later bring in Ben, a carpenter, to make the shelves. But then the committee refuses to pay him, because they say he's too expensive. So, I take Ben and the chairman of the committee back to my house and sit them down with my grandad. "Grandad," I say, "this guy needs paying, and they won't pay him." Grandad, bless him, supports me, and says: "I'll pay Ben." Thus, the committee is shamed into accepting the shelves.

But then they start arguing amongst themselves over which books should be allowed in the library. Four years later, there are no books there. The shelves are used for storing cleaning equipment, mopheads, plastic disposable cups and plates. And the computer? No, that never made it in, either. The committee says that if they brought in a computer, the kids would break it. *That's great,* I think. *If the kids break the computer, that means they're using it and learning from it, so we'll get another one.* But no. The whole thing was a farce and a failure.

I've never felt there was the time to waste discussing things like this. There are too many tasks to be completed, and there are not enough hours in the day – or, in my case, as I believed then, enough years in a life. If things can be changed for the better, then they should be changed. Now. If people's lives can be improved, then action should be taken. Now.

That impulse has driven the growth of Penny Appeal, from its first incarnation in 2009. If we know there are people suffering somewhere, and their lives can be improved with financial support, then we need to get that support to them straightaway. If the charity hasn't got enough money to support them, then it needs to get more money. Now.

What's the most effective way to raise that money? That way? OK, that's the way we'll raise it. What's the most effective and secure way of supporting the recipients on the ground? That way? OK, that's the way we'll deliver it. What are you waiting for?

Penny Appeal has passed many milestones in just ten years. We've changed the way British Muslims think about charity. We've changed the way the entire charity sector looks at fundraising. We've ignored prejudice, refused to saddle ourselves with any ideological baggage, marched to the beat of our own drum – all so our donors and recipients can join together in a meaningful relationship of giving and accepting. *That's* the way we change the world for the better.

There's no time to waste. Not a second.

CHAPTER THREE

SAY YES AND MAKE IT HAPPEN

"Grandad, look! There's water coming out!"

We're at home in Wakefield. It's 1992. I am twelve years old. Grandad and I have just returned from my first visit to our home village of Hathia Dhamial in Pakistan. Grandad is chuckling; I'm staring up at him in wonder in our tiny bathroom, watching water coming out of the cold tap in the sink. Then I grab his arm and pull him over towards the toilet. I press the lever, and the water flushes.

"Look, Grandad! I press that button and the water flows through the toilet!"

He keeps chuckling, shaking his head.

"It's amazing, Grandad!"

He pats me on the head.

"I mean it, Grandad. It's amazing! It's thanks to you that we live in a house where water comes out of taps. It's thanks to you bringing all our family over here to the UK when you did. It's all down to you."

○

I really meant it. That first trip to Pakistan with Grandad opened my eyes. He took me to our village and ancestral home, 50 miles south-east of Islamabad. In Hathia at that time, there was no electricity or gas or running water; there were no *roads*. We took walks in a jungle and I spent time with other kids, trying to catch butterflies, chasing after goats and looking up at camels, trying to determine how tall they actually were. We visited elderly relatives, and I found myself in houses built of dried mud, where water had to be carried in buckets from a well. The backs of kids my age were bowing under the weight of filled water containers, as they staggered back to these mud houses across dusty brown fields. When you carry water on your back, every drop is precious. We used water only when we needed to, and a lot of thought went into being careful, recycling where possible and not wasting any of it.

I couldn't get that idea out of my head. When we returned to Wakefield, I rushed around the house turning taps on and off, shouting at Grandad and Mum.

"Look! Look! It's water!"

That 1992 trip was the first of many visits to my family's home, both before and after the formation of Penny Appeal in 2009. To this day there are still millions of homes in the rural areas of north-east Pakistan with no running water; there are still places where the wells are dry or even poisonous. That's why one of our core campaigns has always been Thirst Relief, providing clean water wells for people all over the world.

After that first visit, whenever money allowed, I would return to Hathia Dhamial. None of the Pakistanis I grew up with in Wakefield ever had what our white friends used to call a "holiday". Getting on a plane to the Costa del Sol, or camping in a tent in Cornwall? We'd have laughed at such notions when I was growing up. The only travelling any of us ever did was to return to our family homes in Pakistan whenever we could, to visit grandparents, aunties and uncles. Often, older family members had the inescapable subject of marriage in the backs of their minds.

Anyway, even if holidays had been our kind of thing, I was too busy as a teenager to think about going anywhere. I'd spent much of my later school days in the art room, discovering an interest and skill in graphic design. If I'm honest, I was never that motivated by the more academic subjects. I'd find myself daydreaming during Maths and English lessons. My GCSE results were all pretty average – apart from Graphic Design, for which I got an A*. That set me on my path, and in time I received a full grant and a place at Newcastle University to study design.

"The backs of kids my age were bowing under the weight of filled water containers, as they staggered back to these mud houses across dusty brown fields."

I lasted a month in Newcastle.

It was the first time I'd ever been away from home, and for all kinds of reasons –missing the family and my Mum's cooking, for one – I could tell it wasn't going to work for me. I managed to transfer my degree course to the University of Leeds, moved back home and spent my student grant on setting up my first business.

I studied design at Leeds, and earned some extra money during the day by working at a pizza shop not far from our house. There I found that the owner wasn't using the room above the shop, so I asked him if he'd let me set up my own graphic design business there. He agreed; after finishing work making pizzas, I'd go upstairs for the evening and set to work on my own business. I soon brought in my first employee: Steve Lewis, a brilliant computer programmer. We'd met through a client project – I was working on the design and Steve was working on the website build – and complemented each other very well. Steve had incredible programming skills, and I had a burning desire to get ahead in business.

Twenty years later, Steve is still with me, sitting behind banks of computers at my main place of business, still eating pot noodles, still looking at me with that wry grin whenever I burst into the

Flava restaurant, Wakefield, 2002

room with a new idea. He was the engineering genius behind the business that transformed my life, singlemuslim.com.

Before long, I invested money from my university grant in converting a local pub into a small restaurant nearby, which I called Flava. It was the first Indian restaurant of its kind. It didn't have flock wallpaper or statues of elephants, but was, instead, very modern, slick for its time, with oak floors and banquette seating. We were also way ahead of our time in being one of the first restaurants to accept online orders. A little alarm would go off in the kitchen whenever an order was made, and the guys would have to print the order off, make it up and deliver it. It was hard work, but I enjoyed the creative aspects too, such as coming up with new dishes. One evening, when we were sitting around the table in the kitchen making plans, one of us dropped a Mars Bar into a curry. Amazingly, it tasted great – as a result, we ended up in all the mainstream newspapers as "the restaurant that had invented chocolate curry". We were invited to Bradford, the curry capital of the UK, to do a piece for a regional TV evening news station. People came from all over the county just to taste the chocolate curry. Mum, natural cook that she is, wasn't very impressed!

I was working every hour of the day now, juggling university studies with running my own design agency on the first floor of the pizza shop, and doing long shifts making and delivering pizzas as well as overseeing the restaurant. Looking back, I can't imagine how I kept it all going. But as you discover when you set out on your own, breakthroughs will come if you keep at it. In my case, the breakthrough came when I bumped into Dave, a salesman at the local Staples stationery store, and cheekily pitched him my company's design services. Whether he took pity on me or was genuinely impressed, I don't know – but he ended up arranging for his boss Brian to come and visit Steve and me above the pizza shop. Brian was very successful, used to employing big ad agencies in London and probably couldn't believe what he was doing – ducking under a pizza counter to climb up the narrow stairs to our office. But he did it, and he ended up giving us a design contract worth £30,000. We never looked back.

What all this crazy activity meant was that, each time I went back to visit family in Pakistan, I had less time and more money. By the time I was twenty, at the turn of the millennium, my new digital business was already bringing in more money every week than Mum earned in a year. Two years later, I was earning ten times that. Like a sensible Northern, Muslim lad, the only 'holiday' I took from my seven-day-a-week work routine was to fly out to Islamabad for a long weekend with relatives.

It was at this point, maybe 2002 or 2003, that the different threads I've mentioned began to merge into one coherent notion: the provision of charity where it was needed in my ancestral home of Gujar Khan, Pakistan.

○

Once a year, maybe twice, I'd get on a plane to Islamabad and make the three-hour journey by car to Hathia Dhamial. The smell, the scents, the feeling, the atmosphere, the heat, the climate, the sounds, the traffic … as the car left the airport, it did actually feel like home to me. Even though I'm British-born, and my home is always going to be Wakefield, this other place felt like home in a different way. It's a feeling that I know has affected many Pakistanis, not just in Britain but all over the world. There are plenty of empty villas out there, built almost on a whim by sentimental Pakistanis seeking a physical bond with the motherland. Mostly, they lie empty, because the owners' lives back in Europe or the US keep them from visiting. But I experienced a great sense of peace and belonging there.

The great thing about Hathia was the lack of pretence. There was none of this "my car's bigger than your car" or "my house is bigger than your house" or "I'm more intelligent than you". You've just come home, that's all, and people love you for being yourself; the older people appreciate you coming to pay a visit, to give them news about family over in England.

On top of that, I felt responsible for taking on the role my father would have done, had he still been alive. I felt he would have tried to do things for his country – and so I had to try and do even more, to include him in the process.

In Hathia, a family would need money to send their kids to school; so I'd pay that, and the next time I'd see them they'd say, "Yes, they can go to school now, thank you – but they can't afford the books." So I'd pay for the books; and the next time, they'd say, "The motorbike's broken, so we can't get the kids to school, so you pay for a new motorbike." When you take action, more action flows on from that. You pay for someone's health care, and then learn that, because they've been ill, they haven't been able to afford to feed their children properly, so they're in debt – and you have to sort that out. You provide the money for a child to go to school, and then discover that the family has now lost the person who was supposed to look after the goat or the sheep, so now that's another problem: you've actually taken away a working asset for that family.

When you start looking into poverty, you see how nothing exists on its own; everything is interlinked. Operating in the developing world, it's easy to think, at first, that you can solve problems by writing a cheque – but it's not like that. The White Saviour/Brown Saviour/Western Saviour complex is a false perspective. It doesn't take into account how cycles of poverty actually work, and how each component of the cycle reinforces poverty, ill health, starvation, mental illness.

My uncles and cousins out there said to me, "Adeem, why are you spending all this money on this person, that person? Why are you taking up all your time? Just enjoy yourself, relax, buy a 4 x 4 and go off-roading, do some shopping, then go back to England. You're never going to be able to help all of them, so why are you bothering to help *any* of them?" I found it difficult to explain my reasons to them. Perhaps back then I still wasn't being honest with myself about what drove me.

As time went by, I had more money to be able to help, but I didn't have the wherewithal to sort out everything when I only stayed in the village for a couple of days at a time. I discussed this with Habib Nawaz, a man who has been a pillar of support in realising my vision. Fifteen years on, he is now in charge of the Penny Appeal operation in Pakistan, but back then he was an intelligent law school graduate living with his family in Hathia.

Habib began to filter requests for me, so that when I did come out to the village, I could see people swiftly and allocate funds appropriately. He and I began to speak more on the telephone when I was back in Wakefield, and on one of those calls he told me about five orphan girls living in a barn outside of Hathia, a couple of villages away. They were literally living in a stable, on their own, with no parents or guardians.

"Why isn't anyone helping them, Habib?" I asked.

"It's not as simple as that, Adeem," he replied.

In a rural community like Gujar Khan, there were complex and deep-rooted traditions about the status of unmarried girls and young women. It was part of the culture of the region that young women should not spend time in proximity with those who were not their close relatives: parents, siblings, uncles, aunts. The idea of taking these five girls out of the barn and into the care of people outside their family would have shocked local people. I asked Habib several times to go and speak to both maternal and paternal extended families, to ask them to come and help foster the girls. None of them would help.

I learned another lesson here: they weren't refusing to help from lack of compassion, but from the impact of poverty. Those families were only just staying afloat with their *own* close relatives around them; the idea of taking on five more mouths to feed would be a burden – and would have been economically impossible for them.

"They can't stay in that barn, Habib," I insisted. "If they want help, just say yes. And make it happen."

Although I never articulated it or even admitted it to myself, I couldn't separate the stories of orphans in my family's village from my own experience.

I realised, however, that taking on such a responsibility could not be done lightly. We would need to get ourselves fully up to speed on issues such as safeguarding and child welfare before we attempted any kind of intervention. Something told me at the time that the whole issue of orphan care could become a major concern for me, so I knew we needed to prepare. Habib discovered a highly respected international charity operating in Pakistan called SOS Villages. They put us in touch with the lady in charge, Fatima, who was head of their Islamabad operation. She explained the process by which it was possible to establish a home for orphans that could meet rural notions of traditional correctness. She also gave us a thorough grounding in safeguarding stages and processes. It was then a delicate matter of consulting with village elders, making clear that safeguarding and Islamic guidance were being followed at every step. Finally, there came the next stage: where to house the girls?

Their names were Rafia Bi (the eldest), Basri Bi, Bushra Kainat, Faiza Bibi and Ghulam Zuhra. Right from the start, I knew that I wanted these five girls to feel they were in a proper home, not an orphanage. I asked Habib to look around the area for a house that I myself would be pleased to live in with my family. Sure enough, he found one in a nearby town called Sohawa. It was new-built, white, with rooms over three floors, and would have made any Pakistani family abroad proud. I took out a lease on it and we gave it a name, "Mera Apna Ghar" – "My Own Home".

The foster mother who had been selected with the help of Fatima from SOS Villages declared the house ready, and the five girls moved in. We took careful steps to ensure that the foster mother was able to introduce the girls into the community, and made sure that the house was secure and safe for them. We installed 24/7 private security, employing a retired army officer who stayed in the entrance, away from the family home.

I felt a rush of happiness when Habib reported back to me over the telephone, describing the girls running about inside the house, laughing, singing. They had begun to live the kinds of lives that every child deserves. Up until that point, I had been offering charity to individuals and families whenever I was asked, in order to help with specific issues they might have. For the first time, with Habib's involvement and with the experts from SOS Villages, I had established something more permanent. I was learning about the cycles of poverty, and this house represented a significant first step in my understanding of how to make real impact. By providing the girls with the stability of a loving home, regular nutritious food, spiritual guidance from their caring foster mother and, crucially, education at the local private school, we had ensured that five young people would have opportunities to grow up and contribute to the future of their country. Who knew what they might achieve?

After a couple of months, I received another phone call from Habib. Rafia Bi, the eldest of the five girls at twelve years old, was unhappy. She had declared her wish to return to living in the barn. Habib didn't know why; nor did the foster mother. No one could understand why she would want to return to a life of poverty, living in a flea-infested stable with donkeys, with no schooling, begging for food. I asked to speak to her myself, but when she came on the phone, she refused to say anything. All she would say was that she wanted to leave. Finally, my mum managed to gently coax the girl into talking, and we discovered why she was so unhappy.

As the eldest of the five, Rafia Bi had always had the respect of her sisters. She was, in effect, the head of the family in that barn. She was the one who held them together, who worked out

"If you're going to make a serious intervention in the life of a twelve-year- old girl at a distance of five thousand miles, then you've got to be prepared to invest more than just money."

how they would find their next meal. This brave little twelve-year-old had acted as mother and father to the other four. But now that role had been assumed by the foster mother, and the five girls were independent. Not only that: as the eldest, she was in a senior class at school, and as she had received no education in her life until that point, she was at the bottom of her class. She had been left feeling worthless. Even her four siblings, still dependent on her, had begun to find new friends and interests apart from her. Overnight, we had taken away her sense of responsibility, adding insult to injury by making her feel intellectually lacking.

Having thus discovered what she was going through, we were able to lessen her unhappiness by making some changes at school and by giving her specific responsibilities in the house. I advised Habib to bring in professional counselling for the girls, to allow them to vocalise any concerns they might have. Of course, they were going to have complicated issues: they'd been living in a barn with no parents! In time, Rafia Bi's despair eased, and she became as happy as the other four to be living at Mera Apna Ghar.

This was a massive wake-up call, a genuine warning. If you're going to make a serious intervention in the life of a twelve-year-old girl at a distance of five thousand miles, then you've got to be prepared to invest more than just money. You've got to think ahead, set up a safeguarding structure that is watertight, put systems in place that don't depend on you, but that can operate for the good of the individual at all times. For the first time, I was overwhelmed by the responsibility I had incurred, and I knew that going forward, we would never be able to take such an unstructured approach again.

The following year, we rented another house and recruited another foster mother. Now we had eleven children under our care. When I went out to visit next, Habib showed me round both homes. I was speechless. Habib kept saying, "What's the matter Adeem? Are you sick? Have you got a fever? Do you have diarrhoea?" But no, I was just lost for words, unable to fully absorb the level of responsibility we had taken on. These eleven children and their futures now depended on us. I thought: *I've done it now. There's no going back.* I had set out to do this, and now it was done; these children depended on me for food, good mental health; their dreams, their aspirations depended on me. Everything was on my shoulders, and my shoulders felt very heavy at that moment.

Despite this sense of burden, I saw that we were lifting orphan care up in the whole district. That was significant. I insisted on a high degree of decoration in the homes, and that the kids had toys – and the very best toys at that. I made sure their toothbrushes were replaced regularly. We had menus so that they could choose their food from a range of locally produced goods. I asked different professionals – doctors, teachers, police officers – to visit the homes each month, so that the children could have role models to aspire to, to motivate their education. I wanted those kids to be as well cared for as my own. Some of the villagers expressed surprise at the standards we were setting in those first two houses, but they were delighted to see these orphans flourish. Our homes soon became the talk of the district, and the standards were spoken about for miles around.

Since working with Habib to set up that first home for orphans in Sohawa, we have insisted on the highest level of safeguarding in all the orphan homes around the world over which we have had direct control. Wherever we've been able to, we've worked with professionals and laid down the clear safeguarding guidelines that stemmed from those early days of hands-on experience managing each aspect of setting up the homes. That vision was based on the idea that, if I died, would I want my own children – the most valuable treasures I had – to live in one of those houses? The answer had to be *yes*.

Another incident occurred soon after we founded Mera Apna Ghar, which reinforced that awareness of the need for broader schemes. When I was in one of the homes a car drew up outside and a woman came to the door with two young and very beautiful children. Their mother came up to me and said, "Take these children. They're orphans. Can you take them, please?" I asked her to come into the office, sat her down, offered her some food, tea and biscuits and then asked her to tell me about the children. It transpired that their father was alive, but serious domestic abuse was going on at home. This woman's husband had beaten her all her adult life, taken the money she earned from her cleaning job and left her alone, battered and bruised, so he could spend her money drinking and taking drugs. Then he would be back to administer more beatings, to steal more. This woman was much older now, however, and had developed arthritis. She could no longer work as a cleaner.

The husband was now just turning up occasionally to beat her.

"I just want to kill myself," she told me, "but I can't – because I've got these two children. I want to drop these children off with you. Then I can go away and kill myself, and I'll know they're being looked after …. Please, take them. Don't tell anyone their story; their father is not a father to them. He is already dead to them."

I had to tell her how sorry I was, that we couldn't take them. Having a father, no matter how bad a man he might be, meant that they would not be orphans. There was simply no way we could take the children in without official paperwork showing that their father had passed away. It broke my heart that we weren't able to take the children in; there was just no way. I have never forgotten their faces, to this day. All I could do was to provide her with some financial support in the hope that she might be able to establish a new home for her and her children.

This deeply troubling encounter led directly to the creation, early in the history of Penny Appeal, of the Street Children campaign. It also led me to discover more about Pakistani society, and the plight of children who actually had parents but not the safety and security of a home. There is no social security in Pakistan, nor any help from the government for low-income families. You are basically on your own. What this means is that tens of thousands of children are left to beg for their families or, worse, are left to fend for themselves. So, when Penny Appeal was more established we started a new campaign, Forgotten Children, for those who fell between the cracks. I never wanted to turn away someone in need again.

The idea of a more permanent charitable structure was becoming inevitable; by 2007 I could see that my personal charity-giving in Gujar Khan would need to be extended before too long into a more resilient, sustainable operation that could scale much more than I could ever provide on my own. It wasn't just that the number of cases in which I was involving myself in was growing; I was also becoming aware of the repeated patterns, tragedies and personal crises that poverty generates. The existence of patterns meant that an institutionalised response could scale well and successfully tackle systemic issues.

○

Sometimes these examples shocked me. On my next visit to Pakistan, I met an elderly homeless man in our village who needed help. That really confused me; I knew in the UK, homelessness was an ever-growing problem, but I had always assumed that the close kinship ties and family support structures of Muslim life meant that, however poor a family was, they never abandoned their own. Families always looked after each other, right?

Habib explained that this gentleman once lived in a village quite a long way away from Hathia. Unmarried, he had some small landholdings that he was encouraged to hand over to other members of his family. He was without money at that point, but his family members had promised they would look after him. Once they had taken over his property, however, they turfed him out. He ended up in Hathia, staying with some distant relatives – who were treating him very badly. They wouldn't let him inside the house – he was forced to live in the courtyard – and wouldn't speak to him or feed him. Somehow, this man ended up knocking on Habib's door, and eventually, Habib rang me up to ask for help. We put the old man up in the annex to our home. He was the most delightful and intelligent person, always smiling, and forever grateful for our help. The last time I saw him, he came around and asked for some money for a haircut. It was always a pleasure to be so directly involved in helping others.

The realisation that poverty could result in homelessness even within a culture I had assumed to be resistant to it upset me a great deal. My own life had been saved in many ways by the kind discipline of my beloved grandad; I was unable to imagine that anyone could treat an elderly person in such a fashion. But I was learning, too, that poverty leads to the erosion of strongly held values. A few years later, once Penny Appeal was up and running, this experience led directly to the creation of the Adopt-a-Gran campaign – set up in the memory of my grandfather Abuzar Khan. So far, we have had sponsorships for over 7,000 elderly people around the world.

○

My education, and my growing understanding of the need to build a more resilient approach to charitable giving, deepened around this time when I met another influential man. Ali was a teacher from my dad's village, Rahoon. I was introduced to him by Habib, who explained to me that Ali's work as a teacher didn't pay him enough to support his wife, children and elderly parents. He also had to travel a long way outside the village to go to work, which cost him in travel as well as time away from the family. Rahoon had no teachers and no school, and Habib reckoned that Ali could begin teaching some children at the local mosque in the village. In order to provide for his extended family, Ali needed £30 a month. It made sense to propose that he should start teaching in Rahoon at that rate, which would allow him to run his household expenses. In 2007, I began to pay Ali. The next time I flew to Pakistan for a few days, I went to meet him.

"Thank you, Ali," I said when we met, "for allowing me to pay my *zakat* to you." *Zakat* is the religious duty of all Muslims to pay at least 2.5 per cent of their wealth each year to the poor

Adeem, aged 19, in Multan

and needy, an obligation that is only satisfied once the donor is able to confirm that the charity has reached the intended recipient. I was genuinely grateful, therefore, to meet Ali, so that I could confirm that a portion of my *zakat* was now being properly received.

Ali is a dignified academic, and a scholarly man. At first, we had an almost amusing tussle, during which we both tried to outdo the other in gratitude – I, thanking him for accepting my *zakat*; he, thanking me for receiving it. Eventually, we had to agree to stop thanking each other. That's when Ali began to educate me more about the cycles of poverty in the developing world. I liked the fact that he knew the value of education. He knew that he would be able to break the cycle and take the next generation of the village out of poverty. The principles I learned from Ali formed the bedrock of Penny Appeal's global thinking, though back in 2007 I still had much to learn.

I learned how generation after generation of poverty can

trap whole families, whole villages, whole *regions* in cycles of poverty that are self-reinforcing. Poverty usually rules out education, without which it is difficult for young people to craft an alternative future. People living in poverty tend to be more vulnerable to climate issues – one bad harvest can result in a whole year's debt, which then means malnutrition, sickness and death: a vicious loop. Poverty denies you the ability to accrue any capital – which means, ironically, that people living in poverty end up paying more for basic services such as health or education, because they have no choice. Poor people are beaten by factors beyond their control, which all have an impact upon each other, worsening poor people's day-to-day lives at a damaging, incremental level. Charities around the world, including Penny Appeal, now see it as a key task always to have an impact on the *contributing* elements of the poverty cycle, rather than merely offering what are, effectively, temporary 'plaster' solutions.

Ali's incredible compassion and painstaking care for his extended family humbled me. I remember flying back to Manchester after meeting him for the first time, picking up my car at the airport and driving to the petrol station to fill it up. I stood by the pump, waiting for the tank to fill, watching the meter: £50 ... £60 ... £70 ... £80 ... £90. The pump clicked; the tank was full. I couldn't take my eyes off the figures on the screen. *Ninety pounds.* I'd just agree with Ali to pay him £30 a month, and for that, some of the children in my home village of Rahoon would begin their education, and Ali's family – his children and elderly parents – would have enough to eat all month. And a day later, I'd just put £90 worth of fuel into this ridiculous car, which I'd drive around Wakefield and maybe further afield for the next week. Then I'd call into another petrol station and put in another £90. For a moment, everything seemed entirely senseless. I felt disgusted with myself. I felt that the world was such an unjust place, and my heart ached for the millions like Ali in so many countries. The name "Penny Appeal" was born in that moment, when I thought of what our pennies could make happen around the world, what our loose change, our pockets full of coins, could do to shift circumstances in life-changing, life-saving ways for others in the world.

○

One more step along the road remained toward the formation of Penny Appeal. At the end of 2008, after returning from another brief visit to Pakistan, I had a meeting with David Taylor, a businessman I knew. He had been one of the first clients of my design agency above the pizza shop. We chatted about this and that, and David – who has been extremely successful in business – was telling me about his recent holiday at Disney World in Florida. It sounded fun: a real five-star experience, with helicopter rides and stays at exclusive hotel resorts. Then he asked me what I'd been doing recently. As I'd just come back from Gujar Khan, all the details were fresh in my head – of the first orphan homes run by Habib, and the teaching work done by Ali ... and all the other projects we were supporting in the area. I was a little embarrassed to tell David all about my village experience – the mosquito bites and the back-to-basics lifestyle of the people, a universe away from the Magic Kingdom in Florida.

David listened carefully. When I'd finished, he leaned over, pulled his briefcase open and took out a chequebook.

"How much do you need?" he asked.

I was taken aback. I hadn't been telling him my stories for any other reason than courtesy. He'd spoken to me of his recent visit abroad, and so I'd done the same.

"What do you mean?" I asked.

"How much will help you in what you're doing out there? I'd like to contribute."

I was stunned. David isn't a Muslim, and he's not Pakistani. He's a successful, middle-aged white Northern businessman who's succeeded in a difficult world, and who likes to treat his family every now and then to a nice holiday. And here he was, offering to contribute money to poverty projects way out of his experience and knowledge, in a country he'd never visited and probably never would.

It was *the* defining moment. In a flash, I knew exactly what to do. It was as though everything in my life had been leading up to this point.

"I can't take your money," I said. "But I'll tell you what I'm going to do. I'll form a charity, get it properly set up – and once I've done that, I'll come back to you, and you can give it as much money as you want."

And that's what I did. A few months later, I met up with David again and, true to his promise, he wrote his first cheque out to Penny Appeal.

CHAPTER FOUR

HOW TO RAISE £100 MILLION

Setting up a charity isn't that difficult. There are plenty of rules and regulations to ensure that good practice is always followed, all put into place by the Charity Commission, the UK's regulator for registered charities. The actual bureaucratic process of establishing a charity really involves three things: employing skilled lawyers to ensure that the founding principles and governing documents are laid down correctly; recruiting trustees who can offer help in areas in which you don't feel you have strengths, and who have good attitudes and share your vision; and choosing a name, a really good name that has punch.

I'd been running a business for ten years by this point, so I knew the value of good legal advice. I chose the best lawyers I could find to lay the groundwork. I also called upon all the strategic lessons I'd learned over the previous few years of collaborating with Habib and Ali in Pakistan, alongside the NGOs we had been engaging with. My charitable work with them had drummed into me how the cycles of poverty were universal laws, not just factors applicable to the Mirpur region. Poverty the world over has the same unforgiving nature, so I deliberately avoided focusing on any particular focus for the new charity. I didn't want us to be 'Muslim This' or 'Islamic That'; in Islam, the principle of charity is universal towards all God's creations, including animals and the environment. I just wanted us to be a force for delivering charitable funding wherever it might be needed, anywhere in the world – anywhere we could make some kind of positive intervention within the cycle of poverty.

I wanted us to be accessible to all. I'd learned as a child what a difference – literally – a few pennies could make to a limited household income. I also knew from the teachings of our Holy Prophet, Peace Be Upon Him, that a poor man's pennies were as valued by God as a rich man's millions. That day when, upon returning from Pakistan, I filled up at the petrol station, I'd been shaken to my core at the contrast between the amount of money going into the tank and the amount Ali needed to support his family and provide priceless teaching to the children of my father's village. As I stared incredulously at the £90 clicking up on the pump's window, I imagined a pile of 1p coins – and knew how much impact even just such a pile could make in the country from which I had just arrived. I remember looking up again at the readout and feeling almost dizzy, seeing the total displayed. *We've got to focus on what is achievable for as many donors as possible,* is what I thought. *We've got to embrace everyone ... we've got to bring everyone on this journey.* If we could request *small change* from as many people as possible, I thought, we could make a *big difference* to a lot of lives. That was exactly how the charity got its name and strapline.

I wanted Penny Appeal to have a life, a character and a future all of its own, I didn't want it to be my private foundation in any way. When Penny Appeal asked for donations, it would not be me doing the asking; this is one of the Five Pillars of our faith, a timeless, Abrahamic desire to help one's neighbour. The proposition, therefore, was absolutely clear and simple from the start, and I intended it to stay that way.

I had plenty of friends and family in both Wakefield and Hathia Dhamial who shook their heads when I told them about my plans to register a charity.

"Adeem," they would say, with kind intentions, "you're not even thirty years old yet. Setting up charities, that's what old men do when they have come towards the end of their lives ... it's a way of giving back for a life well lived. You're doing it the wrong way round. Focus on your business and your family. Let the charity come later."

But they didn't understand. At the age of twenty-nine, I still believed I wouldn't have much time left on Earth. I retained the image from that day when the cars were parked in our street, and the shoes were on the lawn – and although I never mentioned a word to anyone, I said to myself: *If you don't set this up now, you won't live long enough to do it later.*

I genuinely felt I had no choice in the matter. I knew the charitable projects I had worked on with Habib and Ali in Pakistan could be developed further, and I had the energy to create something special to achieve that. There was never any question for me of waiting or delaying; it was now or never.

My generous and charitable client, David Taylor, focused my attention when he honoured his previous pledge by writing out a first cheque to Penny Appeal.

"How much do you plan to raise, Adeem?" he asked.

I hadn't even considered that. I thought for a moment. "A million pounds," I replied. "To start with. Then we're going to raise £100 million."

He raised his eyebrows. "How are you going to raise £100 million?"

"By asking people," I said.

○

Why was I so confident back then in 2009? To explain that, I'll need to say just a little about how I'd grown my business over the previous ten years, because in many ways the lessons I learned and the structures and platforms we'd already built were what enabled me to turn the idea of Penny Appeal into a reality.

Back in 1999, when I'd persuaded Steve Lewis to duck under the pizza shop counter and join me upstairs in my design agency, I didn't have any idea what we'd do. As long as we sit down at a desk in our own office, I just thought, we'll come up with something. Call it the power of positive thinking.

My design degree course had enabled me to get some unpaid work experience at the ITV studios in Leeds, which was my first real experience of white-collar office work. I was fascinated by everything, arriving early every day so I could see what people did when they got to their desks. I offered to make the tea or run over to Argos and pick up a new vacuum cleaner when the one in the office stopped working. I persuaded my mum to make samosas, which I'd bring in to share with the news desk and research team. Their curiosity about this eager little volunteer Pakistani boy sharing his delicious homemade food enabled me to engage with them and quiz them about the minutiae of office life. Why did you ring this person? Why are you having a meeting with that person? How do you know a programme is going to be popular with viewers? How do you know how long a presenter should speak at the start of a show? How does the cameraman know which way to shoot a scene? It was like learning a new language. My only experience of paid employment to date had been serving pizza or stacking shelves in a shop. I had no idea what people did in offices, and I was endlessly inquisitive.

In many ways, it was like that moment when we returned from Pakistan that first time, and I ran around the house turning the taps on and exclaiming to Grandad. This brief period at ITV was a revelation for me. What did I know about the real world, this lad from the terraces in Wakefield who stacked shelves, delivered milk, sold free school meal tokens? I had no idea that people gathered together in offices and behaved in the ways I was so closely observing, like David Attenborough watching a herd of wild animals. Everything fascinated me. What these people thought of this funny little chap hanging onto everyone's words, running every errand he could, I don't know – but the experience opened my eyes and made me realise that there was a whole dimension of human interaction out there, of which previously I had been entirely unaware.

The most revelatory aspect of my unpaid work at ITV – which, because of my eagerness and attitude, continued for a day a week after the initial college work experience was completed – was observing senior staff develop concepts and turn them into concrete projects that would make money. It was like watching the process of alchemy in some mad old film: these people would sit around with nothing but pieces of blank paper and biros, and before long they had invented something which previously didn't exist. I couldn't sit in on enough of those meetings; I almost held my breath while the guys discussed things. After a while, they began to ask me to come up with graphics to go with live campaigns. Even though I was still an unpaid helper, I discovered to my amazement that they were effectively selling my work on for thousands of pounds. It wasn't like all the hand-to-mouth work I'd done before; in business, ideas had *value*. You had a thought; you made that thought come into being through words or graphics … and you found a buyer for what you'd created. That was life-changing stuff.

This realisation encouraged me to think in a more lateral way about recent developments in family life at home. I was eighteen years old now, and Mum had begun to make pointed remarks.

"I'm getting old now, Adeem," she would say. "I need some help in the kitchen. If I had a daughter-in-law, she could help me with all this sewing, and I would have someone to give me some company."

And then Grandad would chip in: "I've only got a few years left in me, Adeem," he would say. "Won't I have the happiness of seeing my grandson happily married before I go?"

I had witnessed enough British Pakistanis heading out to the motherland on holiday and coming back with a ring on their finger and a partner in tow; I knew this was our habit. I understood it, too; in many ways, it is not Muslim behaviour, or the teaching of Islam, it is more of a cultural tradition, from a culture born of rural poverty, in which it makes sense for a tribe to increase its strength by marrying young and having more fit, young people who could work in the fields. I understood where this impulse came from, and I was in no way critical of it; I myself felt that marriage was something to aspire to.

But then Mum started leaving photographs of my first cousins on the mantelpiece or on the dining table, and she would drop hints in every conversation. I couldn't bear it.

"Mum, that's weird. I don't want to marry my cousin."

She'd produce a different photograph: "What about this cousin, then?"

"No!"

Nor was it just me experiencing this. Pakistani friends my age in Wakefield, on my course at Leeds University ... they were all coming under similar pressure. We would talk about it endlessly. It wasn't that we didn't *want* to get married; we just wanted to marry someone of our own choosing, with whom we'd fallen in love.

So, I began to think more conceptually about it, in the way I'd watched the executives do at the ITV offices in Leeds. Steve and I now had agency clients, and we were helping them through the new landscape of Internet marketing. The dotcom boom was in full swing at the end of the '90s, and through my enthusiasm and Steve's technical brilliance, we were making money and becoming proficient in the new World Wide Web. And that's when it occurred to me: why not set up a website to allow Muslims to find marriage partners?

I ran the idea by my friends, who thought it was ridiculous.

Steven Lewis, 1996

"It's never going to work, Adeem," they all said.

"But *I* need it," I said. "Otherwise I'm going to have to marry my cousin. I need to meet a Muslim woman I want to marry. If *I* need it, then *you* need it; our whole community needs it. It's a problem for our entire generation. We all want to find the right person, but we don't know how."

I did my research. This was going to be different to anything else out there. It wasn't a dating site – it was a marriage site, a genuine introduction agency for Muslims who didn't want to be forced to marry people they didn't know. We would provide an Islamically correct alternative to the traditional methods of family introductions and arranged marriages which still respected the values and principles of our faith.

Steve did the technical work on the back end, I

designed the graphics and on 1 August 2000, we launched www.singlemuslim.com. We sat looking at our screens in the room above the pizza shop. Five minutes later, there was a ping. Without any marketing or advertising, someone had found the site, and we had our first customer. He put his name down as "PepsiCola", and he was looking for a wife.

Over the next few months, as we had absolutely no marketing budget, we did anything we could to bring the site to people's attention. We'd type out the URL and a brief description over and over again on paper, cut the paper up into strips and then head out to find people. I remember going to the second Stop the War march in London in 2003, when a million people gathered to protest the invasion of Iraq. We handed out our strips of paper, saying: 'Make love, not war!' I'd persuade Billy and other friends to help me hand out leaflets outside the mosque, which could sometimes get uncomfortable: some of the elders didn't understand or approve of what we were doing.

Within two years, we had over 10,000 people registered on the site. I still remember standing outside a mosque in Bradford in the early days, when the Islamic scholar Sheikh Hamza Yusuf was speaking. The mosque was packed. We were handing out leaflets for Single Muslim, and this giant of a man came over and asked Billy what we were doing. He looked at the leaflet.

"Whose website is this?" he demanded. He looked fierce to me, and I was nervous. I don't mind admitting this: all along, I'd feared that some people might object to this new way of finding a husband or a wife, and I was getting ready for a beating from this huge fellow.

"Brother, I own the site," I said. "How can I help you?"

He broke into a grin and gave me a massive hug. "Thank you," he said. "I met my beautiful wife on your website!"

The website changed my life in every way. I met my own

Adeem receives the Shell LiveWIRE Young Entrepreneur Award, 2003, for SingleMuslim.com

"The whole intention of Penny Appeal was to create a machine that could deliver charity to as many people as possible; of course we would need to be ambitious."

wife, Shama, through the site, and am now blessed with four beautiful children. Within months of launching, the income from the site rocketed; more and more Muslims of all ages discovered how safe and reliable a way it was to find a spouse. Twenty years later, with more than three million members and having resulted in over 100,000 marriages, there's no question that this was a service for Muslims that was much needed – and we delivered it.

As the income from Single Muslim became both reliable and incremental, I was able to start allocating revenue to the marketing budget. We didn't have to carry on cutting up pieces of A4 paper and travelling up and down the country to find Muslim customers. Between the launch of the site in 2000 and the formation of Penny Appeal in 2009, I learned through daily experience how Internet marketing worked. All the buzzwords that get thrown around, mainly by consultants looking to charge you huge amounts of money for very little actual knowledge – *search engine optimisation, clickbait, AdWords* – became part of a vast armoury at our disposal to find and attract Muslims in the UK and, soon, all over the world. Before long, we realised that we had to move beyond

Internet marketing, however; we needed to reach older users who could influence younger family members, and many older potential users were suspicious of the Internet. That's when we turned to television and live events, hosting innovative and often controversial live events such as "Speed Dating for Muslims" and advertising the site on TV entertainment shows.

By the time I came to deposit the registration papers for Penny Appeal with the Charity Commission in 2009, I probably knew as much about marketing a website as anyone else in the country. I'd sweated the Single Muslim figures for five years in that room above the pizza shop, with Steve constantly building new digital architecture for the site. A growing number of people joined our team to carry out verifications, monitor conversations and support me on marketing. In 2005 we'd outgrown the pizza shop and moved into an end-terrace house around the corner, and every day I would pore over the data so that we maximised registrations and, in turn, revenue.

So, when David Taylor asked me in 2009 how much I planned to raise with the new charity, it didn't strike me as ridiculous to put an initial figure of £1 million pounds as a target. I had no idea how long it would take to raise that first million – five years was my guess – but the whole intention of Penny Appeal was to create a machine that could deliver charity to as many people as possible; of course we would need to be ambitious. Single Muslim had taught me how to win at Internet marketing, and Penny Appeal would benefit from that education. A hundred million pounds? Why not?

○

I cleared a desk in Single Muslim's end-terrace offices and made it home to Penny Appeal. The charity didn't have any staff; in fact, we didn't put a single person on the payroll for at least three years. (I made a decision right from the off not to take any income from the charity, which I've stuck to over the last ten years.) But having a desk at least gave the charity a physical presence, and let me focus on what to do next. Practically all of the expenses for running the charity, its rent, utilities, office supplies and so on came directly out of the Single Muslim budget. This was our baby to look after. In 2011 I acquired a lovely Victorian building in the heart of Wakefield city centre to house my growing business. Of course, where Single Muslim went, Penny Appeal followed. We carried on the policy of assuming the costs of the charity but soon the charity started taking more and more rentable space in my building and generating larger expenses. We brought in auditors to review our finances and on advice allocated Penny Appeal a significantly reduced below-market rental rate. One of the secrets of our success in those early years is that the charity was effectively being subsidised and incubated within Single Muslim, and this allowed us to hit the ground running.

We had an official Charity Commission registration, a name and a desk. The next thing we needed was to create a brand. I wanted to use the image of a penny: the notion of affordability was central to the idea of the charity, and was to be accessible to all. I placed the wording PENNY APPEAL: SMALL CHANGE, BIG DIFFERENCE against a copper background with a pile of pennies. But on computer screens, which was where we knew most of our campaign materials would exist, the copper colour of the penny didn't work as a main background; it just ended up looking beige and drab. I laid out the typesetting against orange instead, and immediately, it was clear we had our identity. Team Orange was born!

For me, there was an obvious initial focus for the new charity. We launched it on the fourth anniversary of the 2005 Kashmir earthquake, which had devastated the region, killing 74,000 people and leaving over three million people homeless. Since 2003, I had been giving money to projects in the Konsh Valley district of north-west Pakistan, on the border with Kashmir, so I knew about the impact of the earthquake. A school I had helped sponsor wanted to look after sixty orphan children who worked in nearby fields, but who were not able to abandon their work in order to pursue education. This was a typical situation for the area: young, orphaned children would be taken in by extended family members, but had to pay their way by working – extended families simply couldn't afford to allow them to leave the fields and go to school. The very first funds that the charity received, including David Taylor's initial donation, went towards sponsoring those children to attend the school, and helping the families that were losing those extra pairs of hands in the fields.

I began to feature Penny Appeal on the Single Muslim website and its marketing emails, and started experimenting with more generic online advertising using Google and Facebook. But it wasn't until January 2010 that I had an opportunity to really test how effective these techniques could be for the charity. On the evening of 12 January, reports appeared in the news of a massive earthquake just ten miles west of Port-au-Prince, the capital of Haiti. Within two weeks, the death toll reached 100,000; over a quarter of a million homes had been destroyed or severely damaged, and millions of people were displaced or homeless. It was impossible to watch the early news footage from the island without tears.

We decided that Penny Appeal should immediately ask for donations. It seemed like an obvious next step: the humanitarian case for raising money for the people of Haiti was one hundred per cent clear, and we had just created – although not yet really tested – a new vehicle to attract charitable donations. If the suffering in Haiti wasn't a case for us to support, what would be? We created an advertisement that would have an impact, using our bold logo and orange colour, and put it out across a range of media: it featured on the Single Muslim site and on social media sites such as Facebook, and was plugged into an advertising run on Google. The campaign ran for two weeks, and we raised £25,000. To me, that was an extraordinary result: a brand-new charity that no one had heard of was now suddenly in a position to send aid to Haiti. We were careful, however, conscious of the rush of charity activity in Haiti in the immediate aftermath of the quake; Penny Appeal teamed up with the prestigious children's charity Plan International to use the funds we had raised to deliver help to children in Port-au-Prince. I was thrilled to make the announcement.

This success was repeated once more in October 2010, when we raised £45,000 to aid survivors of the monsoon floods that had hit Pakistan in July. We sent out tonnes of emergency food supplies for 7,000 displaced people: staples such as tea, lentils, rice, wheat and oil were delivered to a hospital in Isakhel in the Punjab region, and to a nearby village called Kamar Mashani. We created the Rebuilding Pakistan Appeal to direct funds towards that village in the coming months, and experimented once more with different forms of marketing-based fundraising. We set up a trek challenge to reach Everest South Base Camp and were inundated with requests to sign up for the journey; each trekker committed to raising at least £5,000 in funds. We sent Team Orange volunteers into Wakefield supermarkets to do charity bag-packing for shoppers. We linked up with Sisterhood Helping Hands in Birmingham on a Family Fun Day, which raised funds for the Rebuilding Pakistan Appeal.

Having spent the previous few years experimenting with my own charitable giving in my family's ancestral home, it was exciting to watch Penny Appeal give satisfaction to people wishing to support those less fortunate than themselves. In a way, it was like providing a service to donors, giving them an honourable, faith-led process to allow them to express their charity.

As a marketing-orientated person, I tried to cover as many bases as possible during these first two years, partly to spread the word about Penny Appeal and partly to learn from direct experience which fundraising activities were more successful than others. I was still convinced that the whole idea of Penny Appeal should remain one of accessibility, such that even a few pence given by a donor would register equally with a gift of thousands of pounds. This crucial element reflected my own experience of life as well as the direct teachings of the Holy Prophet, Peace Be Upon Him. In order to commit to that, we needed to spread our net as widely as we could, to attract as many people as we could. The more people, the more pennies; the more pennies, the more we could do.

By the end of 2011, I'd reached two interesting conclusions. The first concerned our breadth of donors. When we launched the campaign the previous year to raise funds for Haiti, our data showed that while we received donations from Muslims, Christians, Hindus and Jews as well as people of no faith alike, it was the Muslim donors who, in marketing terms, were the most "sticky". In other words, they voluntarily came back to us at a later date to contribute more funds. This was a key insight: it became apparent early on that, while we would grow to become a charity that directed its activities to the needy around the world whatever their faith, we were already clearly a Muslim charity in terms of our donor base.

This realisation deepened for me during our Ramadan campaign in 2011. Ramadan that year fell in August, and we successfully raised over £100,000 from Muslim donors. The campaign was boosted by our radio debut on Unity FM, in which host Na'eem Raza appealed to listeners from noon until *iftar*, the fast-breaking meal at sunset. I learned more about how Ramadan in particular was such a significant period for our donors, and this became my second conclusion: we needed to focus our efforts on Ramadan.

My Muslim readers will be well aware of the Islamic tradition of charity, how it is one of the Five Pillars of our faith, along with the *shahadah* (declaring the oneness of Allah), *salah* (prayer), *sawm* (fasting) and *Hajj* (the pilgrimage). But for my non-Muslim readers, let me briefly describe the landscape of Muslim charity.

The Qur'an tells us the story of a farmer who plants one seed in the ground. That seed germinates and grows into a stalk with seven shoots, and each shoot bears 100 grains. When the farmer comes to take his harvest, he has grown 700 grains from just one seed. Muslims are taught that, at certain holy times of the year such as Ramadan, the rewards for giving charity are multiplied: during Ramadan, we believe, a charitable donation can reward the donor many, many times in the afterlife. In this way, there is a bond – almost a contract – between Penny Appeal and the donor who, by directing his or her charity to one of our campaigns during Ramadan, will be rewarded up to 700 times more than at any other time of the year.

It is a simple but intelligent element of the Islamic system, reinforcing the Pillar of charity and incentivising the donor to give more generously. Muslims give all year round, but with the increased reward during Ramadan and the annual nature of *zakat*, many save their donations until Ramadan, and give extra that month. Ramadan, the ninth month of the Islamic calendar, is special to Muslims for many reasons – not least because it is the month when the Qur'an was first revealed. By fasting during the day throughout the month, and by focusing our thoughts on spiritual matters, we are encouraged to understand better how fortunate we are, and how others may not share in our good fortune. Thus, charity becomes such a feature of the month.

Zakat, as noted earlier, obliges Muslims to donate a minimum of 2.5 per cent of their savings and wealth every year to the needy, and to ensure that the money reaches the right recipient. Until it is discharged in this verifiable way, *zakat* does not register. We were always clear, therefore, that donors could confirm that 100 per cent of the money they donated to Penny Appeal in the form of *zakat* actually went to *zakat*-applicable projects. Many donors generously give more than 2.5 per cent of their wealth each year, and we have always been committed to giving funds not restricted by the rules of *zakat* to both Muslim and non-Muslim causes. But our "100% *Zakat* Policy" guaranteed donors from the start that every penny of their *zakat* would go straight to those who were eligible to receive it.

Charity is deeply entwined in Islam, and there are many strands to it. Beyond the core giving of *zakat* there is, for example, *qurbani*, the ritual slaughter of a livestock animal during Eid al-Adha at the time of *Hajj* – which, again, is an obligation upon Muslims to perform each year. *Qurbani* sacrifice in the modern world, in Britain, is not easy to arrange; in 2010 we launched our first *qurbani* appeal to enable British Muslims to donate their *qurbani* across twelve countries. Sheep, goats, cows and even camels were sacrificed by partners working on the ground in these countries, and the meat was shared amongst needy families. Similarly, *aqiqa*, the offering of a sacrifice for a newborn child, could be arranged somewhere in the world where the meat would prove so important in alleviating hunger in families.

Sadaqah is an optional Muslim form of charity that can be practised both as an expression of worship and as an additional form of generosity. Unlike *zakat*, it does not need to be directed to specific types of recipients, and therefore could be used by Penny Appeal to support many other areas of our work. As we grew, religious endowments such as *waqf* could be directed by us towards the founding of orphan homes. (*Waqf* is traditionally perceived within the faith as an endowment of land or property.)

By the end of 2011, we had identified the core characteristics of Penny Appeal. First, it was bright, brash and full of energy, supported by highly enthusiastic young people who were proud to don the glaringly orange T-shirts. Second, it was founded deep in the heart of the Muslim charitable tradition, honouring the different ways in which Muslims expressed their faith and their worship through charity. Third, it was, and always had to remain, affordable: we were seeking pennies, not thousands of pounds. We welcomed the smallest contribution as much as the highest.

At this point, Penny Appeal was operating out of Victoria Chambers, Single Muslim's splendid Victorian building in the city centre. I still supported the charity by offering it cut-price office space and encouraging my Single Muslim staff to volunteer their spare time to it. No one was actually on the payroll, although we had plenty of orange-T-shirt-clad volunteers coming in to support this appeal and that campaign. We didn't have the infrastructure that developed as the charity grew; we just did whatever was needed to bring in funds to support the early campaign drives in Pakistan and Haiti.

My Single Muslim staff willingly contributed their spare time to helping the new charity. Impressive characters such as David Holmes – "Digital Dave", as I always called him (he was the whiz behind the digital-marketing footprint of Single Muslim) – put in crucial hours late into the night in those early days, and helped build Penny Appeal as a digital brand. The transfer of online marketing knowledge we had built up at Single Muslim was

"Our volunteers put in so much passion and enthusiasm, and so many long hours. That's always been the Penny Appeal way."

effected by my amazing team volunteering their time. Another person who deserves a special mention is Kalim Aslam – "Caring Kalim" – the big friendly giant who heads up Single Muslim's customer-experience unit. Kalim was the first core volunteer at Penny Appeal, doing *everything* long before we even thought about setting up a payroll for the charity.

Penny Appeal was founded with the same mindset with which I had founded my commercial business: have a good idea, then do what you need to do to make it work. Don't take no for an answer. Don't give up – just keep on going until you get to wherever you're going. We were lucky that we had ten years of Single Muslim's online marketing experience to draw upon, but luckier still in the calibre of people who stepped forward, put up their hands and volunteered to help. I've always had a gut instinct for people and on the whole, it has served me well in helping me pick the right team members. Despite being an obsessively driven entrepreneur, I'm perfectly happy with the idea of giving people the freedom to prove what they're capable of. *Teamwork makes the dream work*, as I keep saying. Although occasionally, when a bad apple slips through the net, that dream can become a nightmare.

But I'm getting ahead of myself again. The thing was, back in 2010 and 2011, as we experimented with marketing ideas and responded to emergencies and the needs of the vulnerable in

Pakistan and Haiti, the whole Penny Appeal volunteer team felt the satisfaction of knowing we were having an impact.

There was fun in it, too. The frugal approach we took to everything in the early days of Penny Appeal had its comic moments. In Ramadan 2011, I was the only volunteer, and my mobile phone was the call centre. I took calls at all hours of the day and night: whilst having breakfast, whilst on the road … even in the shower. The number of calls was becoming silly, and when I was with family and friends, I had to excuse myself constantly to say, *"Asalaamu Alaykum, Penny Appeal, how can I help?"* It became a running joke with family and friends who'd greet me with the infamous catchphrase as soon as I turned up. If I needed to talk to someone on my own phone that month, I had to wait until a lull in the donor phone traffic!

Our volunteers put in so much passion and enthusiasm, and so many long hours. That's always been the Penny Appeal way – to keep at it until the objective is delivered, no matter how long it takes or how uncomfortable the environment. The combination of such wonderful commitment together with the growing sophistication and breadth of our campaign work meant that we did finally break through that £1 million barrier in our fourth year, which was actually our first year of full trading as a charity.

A million pounds. We hit the first target I'd originally given David Taylor off the top of my head. A million pounds made up of small donations from a growing number of Muslim donors. It should have been a massive moment but, as is often the case if you have an entrepreneurial mindset, I didn't even reflect upon it. I didn't have the time.

I've never been easily satisfied, particularly with my own performance. If I get somewhere today, I want to get further tomorrow. That's just the way God created me. As I realised we were approaching that first totemic milestone of £1 million,

I already knew that this wouldn't be nearly enough. We had to look again at the potential of Penny Appeal, what it could really deliver. If we could meet a target I'd dreamed up on the spot, then we could meet much tougher targets. But to do that, we would need to broaden the appeal, make the charity's message more vibrant, more attractive, more worthy for far more people. There were changes coming.

One of the people I really relied upon back in 2011 was a man called Yousaf Razaq. Yousaf had raised funds in Bradford in 2006 for an organisation called Human Relief Foundation, which sent money to Pakistan to help rebuild villages destroyed by the 2005 earthquake. Yousaf was a good man who gave me advice at Penny Appeal in the early days; his analytical realism was often a good counter to my frequent outbursts of optimism.

"We're going to do this!" I'd tell Yousaf.

He'd nod and say: "Well, that's all admirable, Brother Adeem, but come and show me when you've done it."

Yousaf had the most remarkable network. He knew everyone; I used to refer to him as "the Universal Adaptor". If you needed to know something about someone, Yousaf was your man. There never seemed to be anyone he didn't know, and that remains true of him to this day!

I confided in him about my feelings regarding the charity's next steps. I told him that we couldn't rest on our laurels, that we had to use our experience to build something much bigger. He's a thoughtful man, Yousaf, and after a while he announced that I should get in touch with a fellow in London called Rizwan.

"I have a feeling," he said, "that you and he might be a good team."

CHAPTER FIVE

TEAMWORK MAKES THE DREAM WORK

Rizwan Khaliq is a sharp-suited, quick-witted creative thinker. Yousaf had told me that he'd been making waves down in London. As the boss of a start-up charity called iF, Rizwan had set a new Guinness World Record with a campaign he'd developed called Gaza 100, back in 2009. He'd asked participants to run 100 metres of the athletics track at Mile End Stadium in East London, raise £100 in sponsorship for doing so and give 100 percent of that sponsorship to charity. He created so much media noise around the event that he broke the existing record by getting 1,675 people to come along and run in a twelve-hour relay. He'd used TV to boost the profile, and managed to get Alan Sugar's *Apprentice* stars to join in. He'd even had a Point of Order in the House of Commons, and with just that one event, he ended up raising tens of thousands of pounds, a fantastic sum which was donated to Save the Children's work in Gaza. A year later, he broke a second record, organising The Big Read at the London Muslim Centre, breaking the Guinness World Record for the number of children reading with an adult. Working with a range of organisations, Rizwan had managed to have 3,234 children read Roald Dahl's *Charlie and the Chocolate Factory* over a 12-hour period. Incredible!

Early in 2012, I invited Rizwan up to Wakefield to find out more about Penny Appeal. My instinct was that I needed help to move us to the next stage of development, and this record-breaker intrigued me. I met him at the train station and took him out to dinner. I hadn't told him anything about my Single Muslim business, and I later found out he had no idea about all that. We spent the dinner going over what Penny Appeal had achieved to date, looking at the metrics of our campaigns and discussing which ones had worked better than others.

At one point, Rizwan looked up at me and said: "How many houses do you own? Have you got two houses?"

He was very direct.

"What if I do?" I replied.

"If you've got two houses, sell them. This charity needs developing. If you've got a third house, sell that, too. I'm not going to start coming up north if you're not committed, if you don't have the money to back this!"

At the end of the evening, as I drove him back to Wakefield Westgate train station so he could make his way back home, I asked him if he would consider coming on board as our first chief executive. I'd observed him all evening and, as I have mentioned, I tend to trust my gut. My impression of this confident Londoner was that he was passionate, sincere and highly creative – but that somehow or other, he was treading water down south. He wasn't making the most of his talents. People tell me that, over the years, I have enabled them to flourish by giving back to them the belief I have in them; that evening, I had a strong sense that Rizwan was the guy I needed to help us expand. I had a powerful intuition that I wouldn't regret offering him a job.

"Let me think about it," he said.

A couple of hours later, I rang his mobile. "Well," I said. "Have you thought about it?"

"I'm still on the train, Adeem," he replied. "I haven't even got to London yet."

"So?"

There was a pause. "OK," he said. "Let's do it. But let's do it right. We're going to become one of the biggest charities in the Muslim charity sector. Anything less than that, I'm not interested."

This was my kind of talk. Although I'm an entrepreneur, and a bit of a one-man band by nature, I've always worked well with strong people who are prepared to argue their case. Right at the start of Single Muslim, back in that cramped office above the pizza shop, Steve Lewis – slurping on his pot noodles

"Although I'm an entrepreneur, and a bit of a one-man band by nature, I've always worked well with strong people who are prepared to argue their case."

– could always tell me clearly and accurately what I was doing wrong. My mum, too, can still give me a good ticking off when she feels like it, which is still most of the time.

Rizwan was perfect for us. He was a maverick, someone who looked at things in a different way and came up with unexpected and often unusual solutions. He wasn't even steeped in the Muslim charity sector, so he had less of the sectarian nonsense to unlearn. He'd worked in other industries for most of his career, and wasn't constrained by the feeling that things had to be done in a certain way. He cared passionately about social justice and the obligation of charity in the Muslim faith – and still does. Our working relationship was vital to the existence of Penny Appeal, and Rizwan remains my fellow trustee to this day, nine long years after he first came on board.

We made an agreement when he joined Penny Appeal: nothing would be set in stone. Between us, we'd review everything that had been achieved so far, and then we'd decide how to move forward. Certain things, I'm pleased to say, have survived that process: the name Penny Appeal, the tagline "Small Change, Big Difference" ... even the bold-as-a-tangerine logo. But as we began the long, detailed process of assessing our achievements to date, it became very clear that the charity was particularly focused on Pakistan – which was not surprising, given the number of projects I'd been sponsoring myself over the previous ten years. We agreed that if we really were going to make a "Big Difference", we had to adopt a global approach. In order to take on that responsibility, we needed to embed a more strategic approach in our thinking. From my travels to Pakistan beginning in 1999, giving charity where it was needed, to the formation of Penny Appeal and its first two years, everything had been done with the express purpose of honouring the Islamic obligation of charity wherever an opportunity arose, regardless of creed or colour. If we were going to significantly increase the level of charity we could offer, we needed to take a longer view of our work. We needed to look two, five, ten years ahead.

As our first real employee, Rizwan represented the new era. Up until now, we'd done everything through the invaluable, extraordinary work of volunteers, mainly in the form of my Single Muslim staff, whom I have mentioned. Now we had someone who could work alongside me to plan strategically. Rizwan joined in May 2012, and Ramadan that year was in July. He suggested that we implement our new, longer-term strategic approach by launching a campaign that he'd conceptualised over the previous months. It was an ambitious plan for the developing world, and it fit our approach perfectly.

Feed Our World launched that Ramadan, and nine years on it remains a key campaign for us. It was a food programme, and thus very much in line with what Ramadan was about: fasting, serving, thinking about how to help those who are without. Providing food is one of the most often-quoted acts of charity in the Qur'an; offering sustenance to those who are going without is fundamental to the faith. Feed Our World was also going to be aimed at ten countries, which would immediately position us as an organisation with global ambitions.

We decided we were going to try, in that first year, to

Adeem aged three with Mum, Dad and sister Zakia, 1983

Adeem's dad's taxi badge, which he never used due to his passing, 1987

Adeem aged five, with sisters Zaheera (one) and Zakia (three), 1985

Adeem aged 19, exploring Pakistan, 1999

Adeem at home aged 21, Wakefield, 2001

Penny Appeal's first teacher, Ali, with his family in Adeem's ancestral village, 2008

Adeem with SingleMuslim.com success story Abdul & Sadia, 2009

Penny Appeal on tour with *Finding Fatimah* movie, Leicester Square, 2017

Adeem at 10 Downing Street to receive the Prime Minister's Points of Light Award with Larry the Cat, 2019

Penny Appeal team hosting Maher Zain in London, 2017

Penny Appeal 10th Anniversary Dinner with Sir Rodney Walker and Lady Anne, 2019

Penny Appeal delivering emergency aid with Mayor of London at Grenfell Tower, 2017

Adeem introducing his daughter, Hajrah, to the future King at Buckingham Palace, 2019

Hajrah, Aayisha, Abdullah and Ruqaiyah at home in Wakefield, 2017

SingleMuslim.com sharing the Penny Appeal story at iDate conference, 2017

Adeem with Mohammed and Basri Bi – Penny Appeal's "Say I Do" Campaign. Helping the poor get married, 2017

feed 10,000 orphans, widows and other needy people in the blessed final ten days of Ramadan, for just £10 and across ten countries, through ten strategic global charity partners. We planned meticulously to bring together a coalition of leading Muslim charities in the sector, chosen for their strengths in certain countries and their proven ability to deliver. Although people hadn't heard of us because Penny Appeal was still so young, they *had* heard of these older, more established charities – most of which had been going for twenty, thirty or forty years, and collected donations in the millions of pounds. They would deliver the food on the ground; our task was to raise the funds.

This was the first time we had applied such strategic planning to the work of Penny Appeal. Until then, we had come up with ideas and delivered them with immediacy and passion. Feed Our World was about coming up with an idea that had the power to spread, to embed, to last. And it was still 100 per cent aligned with our core principle: Small Change, Big Difference.

It was an immediate, fantastic success. Most remarkably, and this demonstrated just how powerful Rizwan's concept was, we noticed that donors returned to give more once they learned about the breadth of the campaign. "Oh, you're focusing on the blessed last ten days, are you? Let me give more .... You're working with the ten top Muslim charities? Here, have more ..."

Ramadan is the month of charity for Muslims, when the Holy Prophet, Peace Be Upon Him, was at his most charitable, his kindest. And it is the month when charity gives back multiple rewards to the giver. The more donors learned about the depth and breadth of this campaign, the more they came back to commit additional funds.

We launched Feed Our World in July 2012 with the aim

of feeding 10,000 people; by the end of the year, we'd fed 500,000. It was astonishing; people genuinely wanted to give and give and give. The campaign became a flagship for us, and we increased the goals incrementally every year, so that by 2013 we were asking for £20 to feed people in twenty countries, and in 2014 we asked for £30 to feed people in thirty countries.

It was ground-breaking. We were the first charity to come in with such an achievable price point: £1 per meal. In one stroke, we'd given shape to the idea I'd first had of small change making a big difference, setting an affordable price for a meal across huge numbers of people and countries and enabling many donors to contribute. The same principle applied to the second campaign we developed, OrphanKind, which had an even lower price point of 50p per day, or £15 per month. When we introduced Thirst Relief, we broke that campaign down to 83p per day, or £25 per month.

This became a key strategic component for us going forward: we were evolving into a charity that was making charitable giving both affordable and rewarding, at a time – in 2012 – when many of the older, more established charities were considered expensive for donors, because they now had massive infrastructure projects and colossal overheads in developing countries that required larger donations to support. Whereas a few years earlier their projects might have needed thousands of pounds, now they needed tens of thousands. They were big, powerful organisations requiring bigger and bigger inputs to sustain them. We, on the other hand, provided donors with opportunities to exercise their charity and reap the spiritual rewards of giving, but at a much more accessible price point. It was almost as though we had become the People's Charity, the easyJet of the charity world. People began to tell us: "I was worried that I couldn't afford to be charitable, to be humanitarian ... I was worried that only wealthier people could afford to contribute ... I was afraid that I just couldn't afford to do good ... Now I know I can make my contribution."

All this pretty much happened overnight in 2012. We were suddenly transformed from a largely Pakistan-centric charity doing *ad hoc* good works in as many ways as we could, to a strategic global charity with long-term, sustainable campaigns. And crucially, those campaigns were spiritual in nature: feeding people, fulfilling the repeated obligation of the Qur'an, looking after orphans, following the Prophet in honouring those who protect and nourish orphans .... These campaigns were highly rewarding for our donors. The Qur'an teaches us that sincere acts such as those our new campaigns offered would be rewarded in Paradise; our donors flocked to support them by the tens of thousands.

It felt as though we had embedded the idea of Penny Appeal into the very heart of the Islamic faith, generating humanitarian outcomes around the world for the needy based on the pennies, the small change, that our donors could afford. We weren't trying to replicate the models of the bigger Muslim charities that had formed years earlier; working together, Rizwan and I were creating a brand-new way of thinking about and delivering charity. It was exciting and daunting in equal measure. From the very early days of my own business life back in 1999, I'd never been afraid of being a disruptor. Single Muslim, as both a concept and a business, always had its share of critics – people who didn't understand it, or who thought somehow it was not appropriate for Islam. But I knew that millions of young Muslims wanted and needed a way of finding their perfect marriage partners; I just happened to come up with the mechanism to help them to do that. In the same way, devout Muslims wanted to express their worship through dutiful and regular charitable giving; now Penny Appeal, in a similarly disruptive way, gave them the opportunity to do that.

During the reshaping of Penny Appeal in 2012, we established a real depth of contact with our donors. They knew, for example, that the Holy Prophet, Peace Be Upon Him, would make an additional *qurbani* sacrifice on behalf of the entire *ummah*, or Muslim community, to make sure that everybody understood the importance and significance of giving and of piety. We're told that when we carry out a sacrifice, it's not the *meat* that reaches God, but your piety. When we make a *qurbani* sacrifice, we are expressing our devotion, acknowledging our connection with God and being humbly grateful for it.

Thus we expanded on the first *qurbani* fundraiser that I had introduced at Penny Appeal in 2010, giving greater emphasis to this important ritual that for so many had just become one more minor formality to arrange. We understood that the act of *qurbani* is so deeply important to us as Muslims; it is a physical expression of our devotion, our faith. In the same way that donors began to make multiple donations to campaigns such as Feed Our World – each donation being an affordable expression of worship – we saw our donors beginning to make multiple *qurbani* donations. With each sacrifice, they could express their devotion to God, and they could also dedicate a sacrifice to a family member or to one of the prophets. And with each sacrifice, somewhere in the developing world, we were providing meat to needy families, some of whom only ever tasted it once a year.

We had created a virtuous circle of giving: donors made multiple donations because they were affordable, and thus they were able to express their devotion that much more often – and earn greater rewards in Paradise. Meanwhile, here on Earth, their multiplying donations enabled us to deliver food and support to the needy around the world at a dizzyingly

Rizwan Khaliq and Adeem in The Gambia, 2014

incremental rate. This directness, this clarity, had never really been laid out before by other charities; our entirely transparent process boosted the confidence of our donor base.

Other, more established charities had tall structures with many layers of middle management and bureaucratic reporting lines. In the space of a few months, we had introduced a massive global feeding campaign with no more than a handful of people working in an entirely flat structure. Nine years on, Penny Appeal retains that structure – an unconventional attitude that seems, in our case at least, to breed creativity, activity and results. We are committed to innovation and creativity, bringing the best of private-sector business thinking into the charity space, turning what had been, until Penny Appeal, a "closed shop" of senior Muslim charities into a more dynamic arena in which ordinary people could feel that their contributions were being recognised.

I found it liberating. Our team was highly motivated by that sense of liberation, too, and our donor base identified with the spiritual benefits as well as our middle-ground stance as British Muslims. There's no doubt that this sometimes put us at odds with older, more established charities that had set ways of going about things; but although we were confident in our approach, we always retained respect for those who had gone before. At the end of the day, these were the shoulders of the giants that had cleared so much of the way for us to be where we were today. Where possible, we collaborated with the best of the bunch. We never set out to upset any of these more

Adeem with Arberor Hadri and Wasim Khalfey, 2013

established organisations; it was actually our support base, our rapidly growing donor community, that pushed us onwards, through their support of our campaigns. We respected the traditional Muslim charity sector, but we weren't in awe of it, and were always convinced that the campaigns and solutions we were coming up with were better aligned with the times. The donors voted with their pennies, and came over to us.

What characterised us was *attitude*: bravado, gusto, appetite for risk. We were a collection of individuals with shared ambitions and values. We were energy-rich, contemporary; there was always a fizz. It wasn't an accident that I'd come up with that orange background right at the start: orange is such a lively colour, and that's what we represented: new life. Our energy was closely linked now to a coherent set of campaigns across thirty countries. Our philosophy of charity was rooted in the notion of affordability and reward – the idea that everyone could participate in our campaigns, not just people with high levels of disposable income. Penny Appeal belonged to its donors; it became the means through which they could carry out their humanitarian obligations.

The strategic commitment we developed in 2012 to our philosophy of giving, of showing our donors that just a few pennies could have an impact if given within the framework of a coherent campaign, allowed us to think more clearly about future campaigns. As we began to expand our role in developing countries, we learned to take decisions based on that philosophy: can we break this new campaign into easily affordable, bite-size chunks? Can a donor, literally, give pennies to a campaign and see a difference? We soaked our entire structure in this way of thinking, and always insisted that everything we did was right for the Penny Appeal brand.

Someone asked me towards the end of 2012: "Is Penny Appeal marketing-led, or programme-led?" It was a good

"What characterised us was attitude: bravado, gusto, appetite for risk. We were a collection of individuals with shared ambitions and values."

question. I had set the initial look of the charity back in 2009 by coming up with the name, strapline, colours and typography. Now Rizwan brought in Arberor Hadri and Wasim Khalfey, the visual graphic-design team at Convey, based in London. He knew them from work he had done in the capital, and once they began working for Penny Appeal, they gave us the look and feel that have given our organisation its iconic yet iconoclastic feel. They allowed us to seem as though we were a multimillion-pound charity before we even raised our first penny. They made us look the part, gave us confidence – and continue to do so to this day.

So, sure: many of the traditional Muslim charities that had carried out such important work over the last ten or twenty years were fundamentally programme-led. We have been very marketing-orientated from the start, and in that sense, you might think that we were more marketing-*led*. But as I thought about it, I realised that wasn't true; we were both marketing-led *and* programme-led. We had created a way of working that saw no boundary between marketing and programmes. In fact, the marketing – which was really our conversational voice with our donor base – informed our choice of programmes as much as our programmes depended on the marketing to fund them. We had learned to be responsive to our donors, to respect their spiritual needs, understand their budgets, be aware of what they wanted to see happening in the programmes we supported. Yet programme commitments were deeply ingrained in our culture, going all the way back to my own involvement with orphans in Hathia Dhamial.

The key thing I remember from those exciting days and nights working with Rizwan and the others at our Wakefield office was the sheer dedication, the passionate determination to be the best charity we could be. Sometimes, when organisations become large, the passion dilutes: you can get brilliant managers, great copywriters, excellent project handlers, but when you have growth, you run the risk of losing the soul that keeps the flame alive. It's a problem that faces all organisations with any ambition: growth presents a challenge. I'll come to how we handled that challenge later on, but first let me describe how we developed OrphanKind, our campaign on behalf of orphaned children, to give you an idea of what it was really like back then.

I had created the OrphanKind campaign in 2011 to support the work that Habib was doing in Hathia Dhamial and Sohawa to provide homes for orphans. Rizwan and I now knew that we wanted to apply the same dynamic we'd seen with Feed Our World to the issue of orphaned children, to take the campaign to a global level and provide long-term, sustainable reasons for our donors to support it. One day, we put together a mini-focus group to talk about it: we all sat around the table in Wakefield sharing thoughts about the issues surrounding orphan care. At the time, in 2012–13, orphan care in the Muslim charity sector really meant education: enrolling a child in school, providing backpacks, books, pencils. That was pretty much all that was considered: orphans just needed to get an education, and then they would have opportunity. Not much else was deemed necessary.

Sitting around the table, there was a real sense that we weren't making progress: we weren't getting to the heart of what it was that orphans really needed. Rizwan said, "OK, guys, let's do something different. Let's talk about *our* children." He asked each person around the table whether or not they had children, what their names were, what they liked to do. He spoke about his own children; I spoke about mine, as well. We all showed each other photos of our children on our phones, then printed some out and stuck them up on a wall. Then we went off to get some lunch.

When we reconvened in the afternoon, Rizwan said, "Right, you've been talking about your Aisha; you've been talking about your Maryam; you've been talking about your baby Mohammed. We've all been talking about our precious children. Now imagine they're all orphans. You've died, all your relatives have died, there's no one there to look after them. They're going to have to go into an orphan programme."

The room fell silent, but he carried on.

"What kind of orphan programme is your Maryam going to go into? What about baby Mohammed? What does your son want? What does your daughter need?"

From that moment onwards, it was a different focus group. Someone said, "My daughter needs more than a satchel with books in it. She likes to have this for breakfast, she likes to do that before she goes to bed. She likes these kinds of clothes, she likes playing these games." We all chipped in with what we thought our children would need.

And that's how we developed OrphanKind. We crafted it as though we were setting it up for our own children, and that brought out the love, the humanity and the affection that we needed to instil in the entire campaign. We had failed to access those values at the start of the focus group, because we were engaging the challenge as professionals. Now we were approaching the task as parents, and that produced an entirely different response.

Today, OrphanKind reflects those values. We don't refer to "orphanages"; we call them *homes*. We provide training for foster mothers, so that they know how to look out for signs of unhappiness or vulnerability. We let children choose clothes and toys just like any child should be able to do.

That's what distinguishes the Penny Appeal philosophy. Unless you can dive deep into what it is that makes us human, you can't know what someone the other side of the world, experiencing hunger or poverty or loneliness or fear, really needs. It's like a leap of the spiritual imagination. As we set about deliberately creating long-term campaigns that could benefit the poor and needy in developing countries, and which could also allow our donors to fulfil their Islamic charitable duties at an affordable rate, we never wavered in our commitment to upholding those humanitarian ideals. Did we always get it right? Not always. Did we make mistakes along the way? Of course. But I know, because I was there in all those meetings, that my colleagues at Penny Appeal were completely committed to delivering the best charity that could be achieved.

Penny Appeal today is built on the same principles we laid out so carefully in the early days, and it will continue to uphold them for the next ten, twenty years. There's still a fearlessness about the way we approach things. We know from very tough experience that things can go wrong, but that doesn't mean that we lose our spirit. It means that we learn from our mistakes and absorb those experiences so that we can ensure they are not repeated. At the same time, we remain as disruptive as we've always been, because our duty is to our donors and the beneficiaries they want us to support.

And teamwork *still* makes the dream work. Those deeply

meaningful programme development meetings we held back in 2012 still inform our work today. We still put faith in our people to deliver as they always have, and I tell you, nine times out of ten, that faith is rewarded. Individuals flourish if you put your faith in them, even if a rare one here and there chooses to rock the boat.

I'm pleased to tell you that the Penny Appeal boat, as of 2021, is full steam ahead.

CHAPTER SIX

CHANGING GEAR

I'm not much of a dreamer. I don't wake up in the morning and think, *that was weird, what was that all about?* I suppose I'm simply a practical, hands-on person, without much time for speculation. But I remember a dream I had years ago, when I was leaving school. I'd been worrying about the future: how was I going to afford a car, how was I ever going to have enough money to get that flight to India I wanted? I was still bringing in little sums into the house, £15 a week for delivering newspapers, milk. How was I ever going to break out of that cycle? Many years later, returning to Wakefield College as an invited speaker and telling the students about how I set up my business, a girl came up to me afterwards and said, "How do you get there? How do you get from having nothing to being where you are?" It really made me think, because I was her age when I started worrying about the same thing.

That's when I had the dream.

I am eighteen. I'm in a country park over the west side of Wakefield called Pugneys. There's a man-made lake there, and water sports; it's the kind of place families go for an afternoon out. I am racing round the lake, going as fast as I can, racing against things that don't move, such as a red telephone box or a lamppost. But no matter how hard I try, these stationary objects are running past *me*. It's as if I haven't moved.

I woke up exhausted. Then, a couple of weeks later, I had exactly the same dream: I found myself in Pugneys Country Park all over again, trying to race against lampposts and telephone boxes – and still losing.

I didn't have to be Sigmund Freud to work out what the dream was trying to tell me: *Stop trying to run so fast, Adeem. Stop trying to do everything at maximum speed.* At the time I'd started university, used my grant money to buy a restaurant, worked at the pizza shop, set up the design business. No wonder I'd had a blooming dream like that! I did pay attention, though; after a little while, once I'd made the restaurant successful and it had been in the national press for conjuring up chocolate curry, I sold it so that I could concentrate on my new business.

I've never lost that feeling, though, that I'm racing against odds over which I've got no control. I deal with it in my own way: by letting people around me go ahead with the way they want to do things. If it works, then great; if it doesn't, then that's when I step in, and that's when people see the less genial side of me. I don't have much patience with failure. I never really knew anything about my dad's way of doing things, and I never talked to Mum about his character until I was well into my thirties. I asked her then what he was like, and she told me that he never used to say a lot, and was always very organised; but when he did want us to know something, he'd yell at us so that we couldn't ignore him. That's a bit how I handle things: because I'm always thinking about the new stuff we should be doing, I prefer to let people get on with it; but as soon as I notice things aren't going well, then I'll roll my sleeves up and muck in and do whatever it takes to help out.

Once Rizwan and I created these long-term, structural campaigns for Penny Appeal, we entered a phase of explosive growth that has never really slowed down. Early in 2013, we passed that crucial £1 million barrier. But my mind was racing ahead, and the following year saw our annual revenue leap to £2.5 million. In 2015, we received almost £9 million, practically all of it from the Muslim community. No institutional funding from big foundations or some super-wealthy individual dropping hundreds of thousands. This was unprecedented in the field of charity, and it turned us into one of the most recognisable names in Muslim giving.

Our workload became immense. Each time we broke one barrier, we created another one for ourselves. The original plan for Feed Our World in 2012, feeding 10,000 people in ten countries across the developing world, required us to set up partnerships with several of the major existing charities with staff on the ground to actually deliver the meals. We weren't expecting the phones to ring quite as constantly as they did that Ramadan, but by the end of the year we had raised enough money to feed 500,000 people. That's a big difference in terms of numbers, so we worked day and night to coordinate with more charities to ensure that there was no breakdown in delivery of meals.

London Marathon, 2018, with Haroon Mota, at the Penny Appeal cheer station

From then on, Penny Appeal was always trying to catch up with itself. We'd set a target we knew we could achieve, and then discover we'd beaten it several times over – and in doing so, created a new problem. These were problems that were good to have; they were problems of success. Even so, they needed careful handling. Penny Appeal never plateaued. There was always another hill in sight, and the way I handled it was reflexive by now: put good people in place, let them be successful, support them as much as possible ... but expect maximum results from them. Usually, it worked.

Part of our phenomenal growth was down to the sheer energy, enthusiasm and passion of our Team Orange volunteers. They really were – and still are – an absolutely amazing bunch of people. For example, my fellow trustee in 2012, Jo Marshall, joined me on a 10 km run in April of that year, when we participated in the Wakefield Hospice 10K race. The two of us were then joined by eleven brilliant Team Orange volunteers, and by the time all thirteen of us had crossed the line – Keith Brook took the honours, with the fastest time of 51 minutes and 44 seconds – we'd raised £1,546 to give to our Clean Water Appeal to build wells in twelve countries. Around the same time, I was humbled to hear that two young pupils from a school in Tring, Hertfordshire had donated £45 to the same appeal after raising the money by running a stall at their school's Christmas enterprise fair. These kinds of contributions happened all the time: genuine expressions of charity by young people in the orange T-shirts.

Now, when you talk about a few hundred pounds raised here and a school sale there, no-one in the charity sector gets particularly excited. *What's that money going to do? It's nothing, right?* Wrong. This was the small change that we asked for and this is what builds into a big difference for those who need it most.

"The breakneck speed of growth was imposed on us by our donors, by their overwhelming response to our campaign calls."

The breakneck speed of growth was also imposed on us by our donors, by their overwhelming response to our campaign calls. I had spent the previous ten years at Single Muslim developing an understanding of how to communicate a simple idea to people on the telephone. Now Rizwan and I focused hard on the style of communication to be used by the Penny Appeal telephone team, brought in for Ramadan 2012.

Remember, our objective was to raise as much money as possible during that blessed month, to deliver as many meals as possible to deserving people around the world. The more money each of our donors gave us, the greater the spiritual benefit they would receive, too; so there were multiple reasons to encourage donors to give more. In order to achieve that, we used proven telephone sales techniques. I believe our team at the call centre was better than the team at Rolls Royce: they believed in the purpose and the vision, and they always went above and beyond. I remember celebrating birthdays with our donors on the telephone, and even sending flowers to grieving families when we lost donors who had been terminally ill.

You could call this customer service, but it was more about us finding out what our donors wanted. How could we ensure that each phone call with a potential donor would be effective? What kind of emotional intelligence was required of our team to manage those calls properly? How could we end a call well? Given that we were talking to fellow Muslims, it seemed appropriate to end each call with a blessing: *Thank you very much; may God bless you and reward you for your generosity. What you have contributed is amazing; what you have done is fitting for this kind of spiritual reward. Thank you sister, thank you brother, your contribution is significant.* Such disciplined attention to detail fostered the right atmosphere and a loyal following, and enabled revenue to surge. Again: small change, big difference.

We were really using call-centre psychology, obeying classic rules such as the Three Ps (Pause, Punch, Pronunciation), making sure that the caller felt properly listened to, varying the tone of voice so that it didn't become dull, being honest and sincere about the campaigns rather than reading off scripts. All our staff went through a two-week intensive training course,

Coventry, street food distribution, November 2018

which we affectionately called "the nursery". They started at the bottom, learning all about Penny Appeal and becoming well informed before being allowed to talk to any donor. They were trained to know how all our campaigns worked, complete with real-life case studies and feedback on how the pennies they collected would make a real impact on the ground – saving lives, changing lives more than we could ever imagine. We were humanising the process. Rizwan and I took turns to make calls ourselves, in front of each of our phone-team members, to demonstrate how these details elicited dynamic responses. We wanted to be best of breed in everything we did, and our incoming phone line – the listening line, the line that would relay our message to our most loyal donors – was no different.

When we launched our 2012 Qurbani campaign it was the time of Eid al-Adha – the time of *Hajj*, which falls later in the year than Eid al-Fitr, the holy day that closes Ramadan. Eid al-Adha commemorates God's intervention in providing a lamb for Abraham to sacrifice in the place of his firstborn son, Ishmael. It is an especially sacred time, and rewarding to donors who, by contributing *qurbani*, are feeding the poor at an immensely significant spiritual moment. We encouraged our telephone donation team to talk about the spiritual origins of Eid al-Adha, to turn the call into a genuine conversation about the origins of *qurbani* and the meaning of providing meat for the needy. This approach, without question, is what encouraged our donors not to give one *qurbani* donation but three, five, ten.

Conversations with donors were structured entirely around our faith, and were based on the Islamic notion that nothing is wasted or meaningless. Putting a morsel of food in a child's mouth is a righteous deed, just as honouring your parents or cherishing your family. God is generous, and the more we act charitably as a means of expressing our worship of Him, the more He gives back to us. I made sure we left on a "feel-good" note with every caller, engaging with them as though they were our family, being genuinely interested in their day and how they were feeling. Some of our calls lasted for fifteen or twenty minutes; however long it was, it didn't matter: we really cared about the donors, and what this act meant to them.

○

During those early years, we became a well-drilled team. Whenever we had a new donor campaign on the horizon, we would clear rooms in the Single Muslim building to make space for an extra team of Penny Appeal phone operatives. Each time, it was like building Noah's Ark, bringing in more desks, telephones and chairs. And when the campaign had run, the temporary staff would leave; the rooms would be rearranged, and life would carry on. From my mobile phone being the original call centre in 2011, by 2012 we had four desks; in 2013, twelve desks; in 2014, twenty-eight desks. Only in 2015 did we finally secure a sixty-person, fully kitted-out call centre that could be extended to over 100 operatives to include the rest of the organisation. This was now the twenty-four-hour hub for all our donation hotlines during the busy periods of Ramadan, *qurbani* and emergencies.

We maintained the flat structure with which we'd started out. I have never worked well inside organisations with tiers of command; I always see waste in them, rather than efficiency. Penny Appeal was no different: if we could spend money on fitting out an orphan home overseas, why use it instead for a fancy office in the UK? Unconsciously, I suppose I still expected everyone to work as single-mindedly as I did, on the assumption we were all on the same mission to raise as much money as we could, in order to deliver as much help as we could.

Until 2015, we were defined by our frugality. In 2014, we still only had four employees working out of one room in the Single Muslim offices in Victoria Chambers. None of the trustees was paid anything. But in terms of rapid growth, this was our tipping point. Various indicators showed the need to establish some more permanent infrastructure, which – reluctantly, I have to admit – I agreed to. My reluctance had nothing to do with any desire to slow our pace. If anything, I grew more impatient as each month went by to see our donations increase, our work in developing countries keep growing. But with the background I had and the entrepreneurial instinct I developed working with Steve above the pizza shop, I developed an innate distrust of job titles, layers of management, processes, traditions. I'm happiest when people come in and tell me something I didn't know, or do something I've never seen before. I believe human beings have an endless capacity for creativity and hard work, and both these qualities can be hindered by bureaucracy. If you want something done, Grandad used to tell me, ask a busy man.

Despite my misgivings, I listened to various people who were genuinely trying to give me what they thought was sound advice at this stage in our development. As a board, we trustees agreed to make some changes.

The first concerned office space. The law of diminishing returns was beginning to apply to the way we would rebuild the Ark with every campaign. The process of fitting out offices with desks and telephones to run each campaign was efficient in one sense, but costly in others; what we gained by not having permanent office space, we lost in extra costs we had to pay to put the structures in place each time. Our revenue trajectory was only going one way – up – and so every successive campaign would need more phones, more desks. My instinct to keep the charity's costs as low as possible by sponsoring various aspects of its running costs through Single Muslim was becoming more and more difficult to accommodate within Single Muslim's accounting. I'd always been clear about wanting the charity to be its own entity, entirely separate from me as an individual or businessman; yet my business fortunes were inextricably linked with the ability of the charity to keep its costs low.

Hesitantly, I agreed with my fellow trustees that we needed to move Penny Appeal into its own space, and we located office space for lease in a building round the corner from Single Muslim. It was like sending a child away to move into their own first house: as much as I knew it was a good 'child' and would do well, I still felt the apprehension that every parent has at such moments. But we'd made a promise from the start to incubate the charity, and we'd fulfilled that vision.

The second change concerned staff. Rizwan's core strengths were creativity, passion and an ability to inspire teams. Since his arrival as our first CEO in 2012, he and I had transformed the charity and given it the programme framework that it retains to this day. We drilled deep into our structure to ensure that every aspect was dedicated towards the raising of funds in support of the programmes we'd created. But Rizwan wasn't put on this Earth to introduce administrative systems and monitor staff appraisal mechanisms. He's a creative, not an administrator – and to that end, he moved sideways in 2014 to become Creative Director, leaving space for someone to carry out the day-to-day running of the organisation.

That person clearly wasn't me. I was still an unpaid trustee, and had my own commercial business, Single Muslim, to run as Chief Executive. I wouldn't have been able to run Penny Appeal as a CEO at the same time, and now with the charity starting on its incredible growth spurt, it needed management. I was happy to retain my influence on its character, and to mentor people as they came in; I was always willing to pass over my marketing expertise to the guys in the new Penny Appeal

"Mum and Grandad drilled into me that if there was something out of sorts – something or someone – then you didn't think about it, you tried to fix it."

office next door. Single Muslim's digital DNA was baked into Penny Appeal's success, so of course I would continue to give it my all as a volunteer trustee.

We had a consultant who had begun to do some work for the charity in 2013 while Rizwan and I were busy building the programme menu. He was ten years older than me, and brandished an MBA on his CV: he'd studied for it while working as a chemist in Nottingham. He looked the part, he talked the talk, and towards the end of 2014, as Rizwan decided to move sideways in order to concentrate on his creative role, the board of trustees decided that we would offer him the post of CEO of Penny Appeal; a decision I would later have cause to regret.

I'm not going to name the fellow. I think you can tell by now that I relish working with talented, positive people, and I like to think that I have a way of encouraging their best. As I've said, I work on gut instinct, and nine times out of ten I get it right. Well, there always has to be a tenth. Let's use the title I gave him once we'd appointed him CEO: "the Sheikh". In the Muslim tradition, the honourable title of Sheikh is reserved for respected elders, senior religious scholars and leaders of tribes. I called him that in sincere recognition of his seniority in age to me, so "the Sheikh" he shall remain.

Finally, the sheer number of Penny Appeal campaigns now

running meant that we needed people handling the phones pretty much all year round. Whereas in previous years we had brought people in to cover the telephone requirements during Ramadan, we now had projects that could be sponsored by donors every month; it was, therefore, much less efficient financially to rely on voluntary and temporary staff. Again, this was really a response to donor pressure. The desire to give during Ramadan was so strong, it became clear that the spiritual benefits our donors perceived might be increased even more for them if they continued to give outside of the holy month. The growth of wider campaigns, which could be sustained throughout the year, thus gave us a reason to talk to donors all year long, rather than just during Ramadan.

These three changes reshaped Penny Appeal in 2015. We were now a charity with rapidly accelerating income, based in its own building, with its own staff and a brand-new chief executive in place to run it. Hindsight is so easy, isn't it? But the charity continued to grow, and we kept breaking our own records with each campaign, and I thought I should play my part in backing the new strategy to the fullest.

A little part of me, though, retained that slight suspicion of job titles, structures, layers, definitions. Throughout my life, it's always been the people who acted naturally, instinctively, who have shown me the way. When I first had the restaurant in Wakefield, our grill broke down in the kitchen one day. There was a chap who owned a restaurant a couple of miles away, whom I hardly knew, and he sent his driver over with a spare grill and had him install it. Then he took our old one to a place in Pontefract, where they fixed it – and he brought it back. I was new to the restaurant industry, and this guy helped me, without my having asked and for no reason other than that he could. Mum and Grandad were like that. They drilled into me that if there was something out of sorts – something or some*one* – then you didn't think about it, you tried to fix it. If the carpet was dirty, you hoovered it. If the swing in the park was broken, you fixed it. You didn't wait to be asked.

In my usual way, however, I brushed aside my underlying unease. *Are you afraid of success?* I would ask myself sometimes, when I found myself dwelling on these matters. *Single Muslim is a lean, successful commercial operation; you're 100 per cent in control of it, and you do it well. The charity you founded, Penny Appeal, has grown up; it's left home, and quite possibly it will continue its incredible growth to become a significant player in the world charity sector. So it needs structure, administration, human resources. It needs all the things that powerful global organisations have. Don't hold it back.*

I gave the Sheikh the respect that his age and job title afforded him. And he brought things to the table, too, such as contacts, energy, enthusiasm. In 2014, as our rapid growth enabled us to consider more countries in which to operate, it seemed to me that Penny Appeal shouldn't just follow the path of the traditional Muslim charities by directing our increased donor money to more programmes in Pakistan, Syria, Gaza – you know, the obvious places. We were innovative, disruptive; shouldn't we start looking at other areas of the world where there was need, other areas that didn't receive so much support from Muslim charities? I put this to the Sheikh, and he responded immediately: *The Gambia.*

It turned out that while consulting for a charity in Nottingham called Muslim Hands, he had been involved with a non-governmental organisation in The Gambia called Annasru Deen and Development (ADD). Why didn't we collaborate with ADD to set up orphan homes in The Gambia, he suggested, where there was an urgent need for them? The Sheikh was already on good terms with the guy who ran ADD, Atabou

Aidara. He could set up a formal link between them and Penny Appeal straight away. In fact, why didn't Atabou take charge of the Penny Appeal operation in The Gambia? At the same time, during the second half of 2014, I had connected with the British boxer Amir Khan, who proposed that his own foundation work alongside us in establishing homes for orphan children in this African country. The other trustees and I gave our blessing, and later in 2014 I flew out to The Gambia with the Sheikh to witness the birth of a new territory for our OrphanKind programme.

Those were heady days. It seemed to me that we were fulfilling the wishes I'd had five years earlier, when I so desperately wanted to expand on the charitable work I was delivering on my own in Pakistan. We were really making a big difference now.

CHAPTER SEVEN

GUINNESS WORLD RECORD BREAKERS

I spoke about time and speed earlier on. I've not met many other people in my life who share my fixation with getting as much done as quickly as possible. It's not a boast, or even something that I'm particularly proud of; it just happens to be the way God has created me, the way my upbringing formed me. I still feel blessed that, when I get up every morning, there are not enough hours in the day to achieve the things I want to achieve.

It became apparent to me around this time that, despite all I'd learned about digital and Internet marketing from my experience building Single Muslim, Penny Appeal needed a broader reach than my commercial business. At Single Muslim, we'd created an online service that catered for a distinct minority: single Muslims looking to find marriage partners. We didn't need to make the Single Muslim service available to a wide variety of people, only those who were sincerely looking for a spouse of their own faith and choice. We didn't need a "broadcast approach" to find and communicate with those people, and in fact by creating too much broadcast noise, we would make it more difficult to track our potential customers individually and offer them our service. Single Muslim was specifically an online service, born in the thrilling days of the dotcom boom, and it has never needed a loudspeaker. To this day, it flourishes happily in the digital world.

Penny Appeal, on the other hand, is entirely different. By 2013, we had powerful campaigns in place: OrphanKind and Thirst Relief were now capable of delivering millions of pounds' worth of support to recipients in developing countries. Feed Our World, set up in 2012, delivered meals to half a million people in ten countries in its first year.

What could we achieve if we opened up our marketing beyond the Internet? How many more meals could we deliver? How many more countries could we cover? Unlike my commercial business, Penny Appeal needed to be presented to *every* Muslim in Britain, not just those seeking marriage. Everyone could make a contribution to Penny Appeal, no matter how small or large; the more we received, the more work we could do in the developing world. It really was that simple. Even if each of the three million Muslims in the UK only gave one penny a day, that would provide 30,000 daily meals to people in need around the world.

○

Back in 2013, however, not everyone was hooked up to the Internet. Even in 2021, there are still large numbers of people in the Western world who aren't online, or who choose not to be. As we hear more and more about Internet fraud, fake news and email scams, it's no wonder that a pretty sizeable minority of the population still prefers to keep their personal lives offline. There are genuine concerns today about digital security, and about the potential erosion of freedoms that some online services can threaten. As a tech entrepreneur, I'm obviously not of that mindset myself, but I'm very conscious that the world is and should be made up of a wide range of opinions and beliefs. I don't think it's the role of a charity such as Penny Appeal to force any particular kind of communication upon its audience; donors and supporters should be able to engage with it on any platform they prefer.

These thoughts led to one very obvious conclusion back in 2013: if we were to reach as many people as we did with the carefully honed campaign messages we'd created, we needed to get on television to reach even more. Whatever their feelings about being online, *everyone* in the early years of the twenty-first century still turned on the telly. British Muslims got their news and watched dramas and news shows from various motherlands, all on satellite TV. That's where they found programmes that were especially relevant to their faith and ethnic origins. That was where we had to go, too.

Sky TV's international programming section was where Muslims could watch programmes, Bollywood movies in Urdu, Arabic, Bangla and more. In 2013, we discovered an opportunity to present on Ramadan TV, a thirty-day pop-up satellite channel on Sky that only ran for the month. It was very popular in the Muslim community, because although some of the other channels catered for Ramadan, none of them gave themselves over exclusively to it. It's hard to underestimate how important Ramadan is in the Muslim calendar. Everything for the believer is transformed in this month. I found out that it was possible to pay for advertisement slots on the channel. And so we did, on the fourth, thirteenth and twenty-seventh nights of Ramadan, the last being the most important night of the holy month. The team and I did some calculations, working out what we would need to raise in terms of donations to make our expenditure on a TV presence worthwhile. Quite a few other Muslim charities had already bought airtime on Ramadan TV; it was clearly a method of communicating with the donors at home in their own living rooms.

They'd had some technical problem with the station that year, or maybe it was just Asian timing: they had only gone live on the third night of Ramadan, and the charities that presented that night had only brought in about £2,000 in donations. We came in the following night, and rocked up at the studios in London with our presenters, volunteers, banners, campaign themes. The station organisers tried to manage our expectations, telling us not to get our hopes up too much, but I was thinking: *I've done the calculations; we know this can be an effective way of raising funds for our projects. I'm not going to accept failure. We're not investing the charity's money on airtime without being sure we'll make it back.*

What the organisers didn't know was that we'd already done what effective marketing organisations do, and had tuned in our entire Single Muslim and Penny Appeal databases to the news that we were going to appear on Ramadan TV on the fourth night. We'd emailed all our existing donors to let them know, asking them to tune in on the night with family members, and to tell their friends to tune in. We sent text messages out to all the numbers we had, we placed web adverts. We did everything we could to activate our donor base. I told everyone connected with Single Muslim to spread the word: tune in to Ramadan TV at such-and-such time on the fourth night of Ramadan, and give generously!

That first night was a complete shocker for me. We received phone calls while the show was live. I was monitoring the calls, and what really amazed me was when I suddenly realised, *hold on, that's my auntie from Dewsbury; wait a minute, that's my uncle from Birmingham … that's my cousin from Wembley.* I had been telling them about Penny Appeal for the last three years and they'd not donated; all of sudden, now they did. I spoke to my auntie that night and she said, "Well, Adeem, Penny Appeal is a proper charity now, isn't it? You're on TV. I'm so proud of you, and that's why I gave my money."

We also saw people respond to the TV appeal whom we had never reached before. That first night we were on, after the charities that had been on the previous day had raised only £2,000, we raised £30,000; on the thirteenth night, we doubled that to over £60,000; on our last night, we doubled it again to a tremendous £120,000-plus, all to help the neediest around the world. I was told other charities were still only doing £3,000 or £4,000 on their nights on the same channel. The difference was obviously something to do with the character and calibre of our presenters: we had Yusuf Estes over from the US; Rashid Khan from Channel 4's hit TV series *Make Bradford*

"Call now – pick up the phone: zero three thousand eleven eleven eleven!"

British; the legendary Ahmad Bostan from Birmingham; Ahmad Dabche from Syria Relief; and Rizwan Khaliq put in a powerful performance. They were all sincere, brilliant communicators.

We had also meticulously planned and prepared ourselves for those three nights, and executed them with precision, in addition to having pre-marketed to absolutely everyone we knew. We'd rehearsed endlessly. We also made sure that the telephone number we were asking people to phone in on was memorable: 03000 11 11 11. *Call now – pick up the phone: zero three thousand eleven eleven eleven!* We just kept saying it all night. It worked so well that every time one of the presenters mentioned the number, guess what? We'd get a phone call. I was in the gallery, in contact with our temporary call centre back in Wakefield. We had four people on the phones there, and every time they told me they had no calls, I'd get a message through to one of the presenters' earpieces, asking them to mention the number. They'd do it, and the calls would start again. When the call centre told me all the phones were busy, I'd tell the presenters *not* to mention the number. When the calls came to an end, I'd be back into the presenters' earpieces. It went on like that for eight hours.

After that successful experience, I told everyone we needed to increase the number of nights we were on television. It was so evidently successful for the charity; we needed fifteen nights, not three. The multiple of donations versus airtime cost was so dramatic that there was no question. So we tried all the other Muslim TV stations again, including Islam Channel, Noor TV and Iqra TV, trying to book much more airtime for Ramadan 2014. But no one would let us in; they all told us they were too busy, too booked up. In some sense, I think we were running up against the problem I've already described: we were considered rather young, brash, unconventional, and few of the traditional Muslim networks welcomed us. There was a little bit of that "closed shop" mentality: serve your time, wait in line.

Well, as you know, waiting has never been my strong point. "There's nothing else for it," I said to my fellow trustees at Penny Appeal, "we need to find someone who we can work with and shares our vision to showcase what real British Muslim life is about, not make the kind of TV that our elders want us to resemble." Remember, Single Muslim had no need of TV: we'd never explored that before on the commercial side. But it was clear now that Penny Appeal *was* going to depend on growing access to a TV audience.

As luck would have it, I'd been speaking to a smart young engineer at Sky during our 2013 shows, a guy called Arshad Ashraf, ("Ash" for short). I'd been telling him about the problems we faced getting airtime, and said to him, "Look, I think I could get two or three other Muslim charities and several Muslim businesses to agree to advertise on a new Muslim TV station." At the time, there was only one other English-language Muslim TV channel, Islam Channel; all the others were foreign-language. Islam Channel already had ten charities working with it, which was their full charity capacity. So I knew there was an opening for a second Muslim English-language station. Ash agreed, and told me about his desire to set up a TV station for a British Muslim audience. He reeled off a million ideas for programmes, and a long list of the steps Muslims needed to take to work in arts and media, establish our identity as a community in the West and shape our cultural narrative. He was a very deep thinker, and I liked that. Within four months, the aptly named British Muslim TV, BMTV for short, had been born.

Penny Appeal was careful not to involve itself in setting up or running the station. BMTV needed to be an entirely independent, commercial television station that would be receptive to our requests to book airtime for appeals. We needed an absolutely clear dividing line between the TV station selling airtime and Penny Appeal buying it. Eight years later, BMTV continues to flourish under Ash's leadership. It remains independently owned, and has proved invaluable in growing the Penny Appeal brand. That's how we do things at Penny Appeal: once we've found something that works, such as TV campaigning, then we'll scale it up and up and up until we hit the sweet spot to ensure we're getting the maximum return on our investment and having maximum impact through the great work we're doing. Why wouldn't we? In the early years, BMTV contributed to as much as 50 per cent of Penny Appeal's annual revenue; in later years, as Penny Appeal grew, it was still as much as 20 per cent of our annual turnover.

I'll come back to this point several times. Penny Appeal has never been wary of spending money when that money brings in even more funds that we can allocate in the field. This is evident in our growth, and in the increase in spending on programmes. In 2013, as soon as we saw the results of those three nights on Ramadan TV – over £200,000 from an airtime investment of £20,000, a whopping *ten times* return on investment – I knew we had to spend money booking at least five times the number of nights the following year. It's a very simple marketing equation: you find a medium in which your audience feels comfortable and confident; purchase access to them via that medium; present an honest and sincere set of charitable programmes; and engage donors with live appeals they can call in to. Then you benefit from dramatically increased donations. I'm not remotely ashamed of the money the charity has spent advertising its campaigns; without it, we wouldn't have been able to help so many people and save so many lives across the world.

Over the years, we have had critics – often anonymous and online ("keyboard warriors", as we call them) – complain that Penny Appeal invests a lot of money on TV airtime. They don't seem to mind so much when other charities do likewise on other stations. But when Penny Appeal invests in airtime to reach its audience, and when that investment brings in huge multiples of donations, contributing directly to our astronomical growth, then somehow that's not quite right. I've never understood it. TV appeals represented a better return on investment than, say, hosting a fancy gala dinner and bringing a big celebrity guest. Once you've tallied up the cost of the venue, the food, the talent, you end up spending a lot of money. Even when we explained this to detractors, they still weren't happy. Mum tells me it's because I'm too young: "If you had started Penny Appeal when you were a sixty-year-old grandad, Adeem, then people wouldn't have criticised you. You started so young. You still have a full head of hair."

Well, Mum, you know how it was. There wasn't time.

Keeping BMTV at arm's length, I worked like crazy with Ash so that it would be ready for Ramadan 2014. If I'm honest, we actually started off by buying a second-hand book from eBay titled *How to Build a TV Station*. I was like, "Guys, What's a satellite uplink? What do we need that for? What's an Ofcom licence? What does a transponder do?" Ash soon told me that my extensive technical abilities would actually only get in the way; to this day, I don't really know how he managed to do it. He built a TV station with its own studios in Victoria Chambers. We negotiated successfully to get airtime on Sky TV, and BMTV went live in June 2014.

After all the knockbacks from the existing Muslim TV stations, telling us that we couldn't buy the airtime we needed to fundraise for our campaigns, Penny Appeal now had access to a friendly, local Muslim TV station that would permit the charity to access *half* its airtime, and was free of the sectarian and traditional baggage that all the others had. BMTV put us in Muslim households seven days a week. Looking back, it is one of the main reasons Penny Appeal was able to become a household name. If I hadn't pushed and pushed, and if Ash hadn't worked his technical miracles, we'd have been stuck with just three nights again for Ramadan 2014. Instead, as you'll discover, we managed to get quite a bit more airtime than that.

During this period, I'd taken a couple of family holidays to Dubai. Amongst many other observations, I'd noticed how popular the Guinness World Records tradition was out there. It seemed the Islamic world was fascinated by how many different ways people could push the human physical and mental spirit and break records. When I came back to Wakefield, I asked my family about it: they all agreed that the Guinness World Records TV shows were big favourites. I loved them too; everyone did. Knowing all these facts and figures, wondering who was going to break the next record, seemed to tickle people. I thought: *Penny Appeal should break the fundraising record.*

There was a standout record for us to challenge: the longest televised charity appeal. Penny Appeal would benefit, because we'd be maximising our donations, and it would benefit Ash's

GUINNESS
WORLD RECORDS

CERTIFICATE

The longest live broadcast
for a charitable event
was achieved by
Penny Appeal (UK)
at British Muslim TV Studios
in Wakefield, UK
from 2 July to 14 July 2015

OFFICIALLY

RECORD HOLDER

Amir Khan (left) with the Guinness World Record
blue blazer at the British Muslim TV studio and
Arshad Ashraf (right) with Adeem, 2015

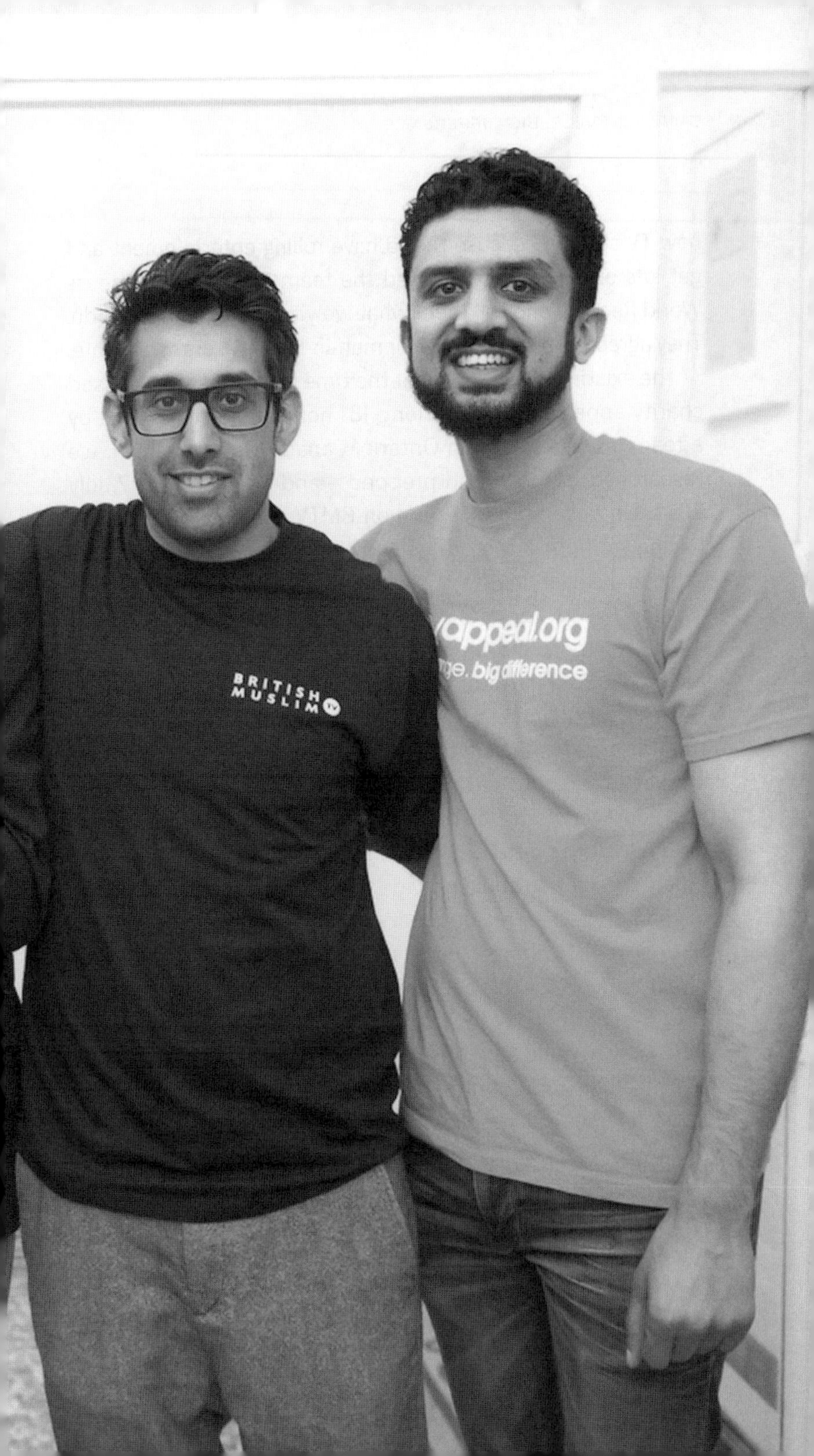
BRITISH
MUSLIM
big difference

new TV station, because they'd have rolling entertainment and get lots of exposure. We asked the team to contact Guinness World Records and tell them what we were going to try and do. They agreed to send one of their men-in-blue-blazers to officiate.

The existing world record at the time for a nonstop televised charity appeal was a superlong 181 hours, held since 2001 by a team in Mississauga in Ontario, Canada. So once again, we researched, planned and prepped – and on Thursday 17 July 2014, we began broadcasting on BMTV, the Guinness people having verified all the timers and checked they were in place. We had a stellar line-up of presenters: Ahmad Bostan, Rizwan Khaliq, Jawad Sarwar, Imran Safdar, Alyas Karmani, Imam Ajmal Masroor, Shaykh Reda Bedeir, Sheikh Abdur-Raheem McCarthy, Shaykh Abdullah Hakim Quick, Sister Aala live from Gaza, Yusuf Chambers. This was the Premier League of Muslim fundraisers. Moreover, the Gaza emergency was unfolding at that time, and there was a serious need for funding. We had footage of the terrible events taking place there, and detailed all the different ways in which our programmes and emergency action could provide help. The presenters did what we had done the previous year on Ramadan TV, repeating the 03000 11 11 11 number constantly and intercutting that with direct appeals for this campaign and that: 16p a day for Open Your Eyes, 50p a day to sponsor an orphan with OrphanKind, 82p a day to build a well as part of Thirst Relief, £10 to deliver ten meals in ten countries under Feed Our World, £150 or £300 for medical supplies for Gaza, £50 for a food pack for Gaza. We had a studio packed with people, all chanting, *"In Our Thousands, In Our Millions, We Are All Palestinians!"* The team just didn't stop; the enthusiasm and the energy and the sincerity were incredible.

After seven full days, seventeen hours and seven minutes, we looked at the clock and realised we'd done it: we'd been on

"We had made so much noise over those seven days, it was impossible for anyone in the British Muslim community not to know about Penny Appeal."

air for 185 hours non-stop, four hours longer than the previous record. We were exhausted, thrilled, emotional. The man in the blazer from Guinness had returned to oversee the final hours, and I turned to him, triumphant: "We've done it!" I cried.

"I'm not sure," he said.

"What do you mean, 'you're not sure'?" I replied. "We've been on air for 185 hours, we've smashed the record, you were here to see it. What do you mean 'you're not sure'?"

He was just doing his job. Patiently, he sat down with the tech guys and went over all the statistics showing how long we'd been on air. After what seemed like days – but was probably no more than an hour – he stood up.

"Congratulations," he said in a very official voice. "Penny Appeal is confirmed as the Guinness World Record holder for the longest live TV charity appeal!"

The studio went crazy, everyone laughing and crying and praying.

We raised £1,187,372 in those seven days. Let me repeat that: in seven days, Penny Appeal received over *one million pounds* in donations. It was unheard of. We had made so much noise over those seven days, it was impossible for anyone in the British Muslim community not to know about Penny Appeal. Most of that £1.1million came in over the phone lines; some of it came through the post; but *none* of it would have come in without the astonishing impact of that week of broadcasting.

We became known to everyone as the 'charity that had broken the Guinness World Record'. The Guinness World Record programmes were an easy but memorable bit of fun. There are Guinness World Records for the most burgers eaten, the most expensive car, the largest number of bricks smashed with a kick. If the record-breaking was already a hit with the British Muslim community, here we were breaking a record to provide food for starving people, providing clean water, education, for people in need, taking a light-hearted entertainment and turning it into something that was all about saving lives and improving conditions for millions of people.

For Penny Appeal, this was transformative. We were suddenly seen by aunties and uncles as *the* British Muslim charity, sending money to Gaza, Pakistan, Syria, running clear and sustainable programmes to help orphans, provide clean water wells, feed hungry families, fix failing eyesight. For so many people to be able to see these issues being tackled on TV, to watch a mix of entertainers and inspirational spiritual leaders come together to tackle the problem of global poverty ... this changed the way Penny Appeal was understood by donors. Without that record-breaking show, we would never have broken through the donations barrier so quickly. We would never have been able to deliver so much charitable activity around the world. I couldn't have been prouder of Team Orange.

Oh, and I almost forgot: the following year, we thought we'd try and break our own record. And we did. At 4.11 AM on 14 July 2015, we set a new Guinness World Record for the longest live charity TV broadcast – an incredible eleven days, eleven hours and eleven minutes on British Muslim TV, raising £1,641,270. *Zero three thousand eleven eleven eleven!* – just in case you missed it – was probably the most-mentioned phone number on any British satellite TV channel.

As I kept saying to everyone in Team Orange, and as I keep saying: it's teamwork that makes the dream work.

Penny Appeal breaking the Guinness World Record, 2015

CHAPTER EIGHT

IMPOSSIBLE SPELLS I'M POSSIBLE!

My mum taught me most things about life. By doing what she told me when I was a lad, I helped her survive the tough task of raising a family on her own. There wasn't room in our house in Wakefield for ego – or for rebellion, for that matter. Only she will know what she really went through all those years bringing us up, but I knew instinctively that it was support she needed, not teenage kicks.

I chose, at quite a young age, to be an observer, and to listen. More than anyone else, Mum showed me *by example* how to grow financially, one step at a time. She was very unusual in the Pakistani community of Wakefield in the 1990s, being the sole breadwinner in a house with three kids and a poorly parent. From her piecework sewing jobs to acquiring her car and thus her independence, renting a market stall and then opening her own shop, I now realise that every step of her courageous progress involved calculated risk. She had to weigh up what she'd achieved, count the pennies she'd saved and work out what she needed to invest to build a more solid future for her family. Month after month, year after year, Mum was a case study in diligent entrepreneurial thinking.

As she struggled so hard to keep our family together, I remember the wise words of my grandad one morning when I showed some reluctance about making my bed: "Adeem, look at your mother; see how she works. If you keep going, then you have a chance. You might not win, but by keeping going, you are still in the game. If you give up, if you walk off the pitch, then you have no chance of winning."

These simple words have stayed with me. *If you give up, you have no chance.* If you keep going, then the odds begin to turn your way.

Mum's lessons in frugality have always stayed with me, too. You can't expand if you don't invest for the future, but you won't *have* a future if you fritter your money away on non-essential things. These are two crucial factors for the long-term health of any organisation, whether you're a single-parent family struggling to keep your head above water or a commercial business or a charity. They are rules I have kept to, scrupulously, in Single Muslim, which still operates successfully on a very lean model with relatively low administrative overheads. We're still using the same desks, chairs and teapots we've always used.

However, at some point in the life of every organisation, you've got to buy those desks, chairs and teapots. You've got to invest in the future. They don't appear out of nowhere. So, when we moved Penny Appeal to its own rented offices in 2015, we had to commit expenditure to kitting out the charity for the future. Five years on, as I write this, we're still doing very nicely with a lot of the equipment and materials we purchased back then. It's a really important point: when you buy a desk to allow a member of staff to work effectively, you don't then buy them another desk the following month. They use that desk for years. It's a long-term investment. For some reason, though – and I tend, in my usual way, not to reflect too deeply on what that reason might be – we began to encounter criticism by a small and apparently bitter minority that accused us of spending too much money on set-up and administration costs.

One online forum published some ill-informed criticism of us in this respect, towards the end of 2015. We were wrongly accused of having inflated overhead spends and of holding back funds from donations. To his credit, the newly installed CEO – the Sheikh – replied in public on behalf of the charity:

> We intentionally held what seems like a large proportion in the charity reserves simply because we were at the start of a major construction programme in The Gambia. Ten orphan homes, a Masjid and an administration block. Anyone who knows anything about building and

contractors will be able to tell you that you shouldn't give all the money up front, you should release it at pre-defined milestones, and you should also be careful not to run out of money as if contractors leave your site, getting them back is a nightmare. This was a £750,000 project.

Every Ramadan we also have our annual Feed Our World Programme. In Ramadan 2014 we expanded to 30 countries and fed 1 million meals. A significant logistical undertaking which also required pre-Ramadan cash flow.

All charities receive such criticism. It comes with the territory, particularly when you are a game-changing organisation like Penny Appeal. You get the haters: often anonymous individuals who use social media as camouflage, and the Internet to spread false information about us. All we can do is to remind ourselves of the wise tradition of the Holy Prophet, Peace and Blessings Be Upon Him, who said: "It is enough of a lie for people if they speak on everything they hear."

○

Everything was changing for us. The donations breakthrough we achieved in 2014 had allowed us to put in place the strategy we had developed two years earlier. We had the campaigns prepared and done immense amounts of research. We knew where aid was needed. But we had needed access to the level of Muslim charitable donations to be able to put those programmes to work. With our move into television, our record-breaking and our rapidly spreading Team Orange public profile, we were good to go.

Nothing would be the same again. From May 2014 to April 2015, our revenue exploded to just under £9 million from £2.5 million the previous year. This kind of growth was unprecedented in the Islamic charity sector – in fact, in the entire British charity sector. We were ready for it; we had planned for it, and we knew how to allocate it. But some people didn't like to see such a meteoric rise.

The lessons of my mum's frugality were always uppermost in my mind; on top of that, the responsibility of taking donations from devout supporters always weighed very heavily on me. So, it was important for us to have clear methods of financial planning and control.

First, we imposed the "100% Zakat Policy", which Penny Appeal retains to this day. *Zakat*, as discussed earlier, is one of the Five Pillars of Islam, the commandment from God to believers to offer up at least 2.5 per cent of their wealth to charity each year. *Zakat* is emphasised both in the Qur'an (where it is mentioned thirty-two times) and the *Sunnah*. For Muslims, the power of *zakat* cannot be underestimated; it is in itself an expression of faith. Devout Muslims must be able to verify that their *zakat* has been given correctly. Years before, when I thanked Ali in Hathia for allowing me to give my *zakat* to him, I was able to see clearly where my charity was going. The 100% Zakat Policy reassured our Muslim donors that every single penny of their *zakat* donation would go directly to those who needed it most, 100 per cent of the time, to *zakat*-approved programmes; that they could expect 100 per cent verification – and that they would receive 100 per cent of the reward.

The word *zakat* comes from the Arabic root signifying 'purity', 'increase', 'blessing' and 'praise'. It was fundamental to us that we build the new, growing Penny Appeal upon a solid and true spiritual foundation.

All donations over and above an individual's 2.5 per cent *zakat* contribution can be used to develop the complete range of our activities, and can also be allocated towards the development of future programmes – so, for example, we might choose to hold funds in Penny Appeal's accounts from one year to the next, so that we knew we had sufficient revenue to book airtime during Ramadan. Or we might allocate funds to fitting out a call centre, so that we could increase the number of donations we were able to accept. These are areas where sensible business practice impinges upon the notion of charity – in my view, in a very positive way – because the charity ends up being better structured, stronger and more durable, which in turn means that it is able to deliver charity more widely and more effectively going forward. We have become a remarkably efficient distributor of charity, thanks to the sure foundations we laid back then.

We needed a securely funded (if modest) central administration in Wakefield, because as the levels of donations began to rocket, we had to ensure that delivery in the field remained seamless. From 2012 to 2014, we had created a series of programme campaigns that were resilient and sustainable enough to accommodate significant revenue rises without compromise on the delivery. Feed Our World, the campaign we developed and first introduced in July 2012, is a perfect case in point. In its inaugural year, we planned to provide 10,000 meals across ten countries; we ended up providing 500,000 meals. The following year, we aimed to deliver 600,000 meals across twenty countries, and ended up delivering almost 800,000 meals. For 2014, the year of our Guinness World Record, we had set a target for Feed Our World of one million meals across thirty countries during Ramadan; we ended up providing 3,235,852 meals during the whole of 2014. That meant that on more than three million occasions, people in need in thirty countries did not have to worry about where their next meal would come from.

In other words, though our donations had catapulted, we had

already built a programme structure that could accommodate whatever revenue we attracted, through partnerships with long-standing, proven organisations. They had people on the ground in the thirty countries where we wanted to make a difference, and they were able to accept our funds and deliver the meals to those most in need. This allowed us to empower local communities and local actors without us having to build large and expensive competing structures all over the world – which I have always regarded as wasting resources that are much better spent on providing actual aid. Setting up and managing all those relationships with important delivery partners required a motivated, talented and effectively funded team back at base. We were a long, long way from Adeem Younis going around to his mum's house for tea in 2011 and taking donation calls on his mobile phone in between conversations. Now, only four years later, we had one of the most effective call centres in the North of England.

So: no, I have no qualms at all about having set up our office properly. As I have said, you'll find all the desks and chairs we bought in 2015 still in use today.

To put it all into context, please indulge me for a moment as I tell you how our work abroad began to magnify at this point. The facts and figures I'll give below have been overtaken many, many times since 2015, but they give an idea of how the landscape was changing at the time.

Feed Our World has become one of the most successful UK-based charitable food programmes. And it is based on the simple principle of "small change, big difference". Of the 3.2 million meals we distributed in 2014, 18 per cent of them were given out to individuals suffering in some kind of emergency;

37% were given out at Ramadan; and 45% were given out during the rest of the year as required. It's enlightening to look at whom those meals went to. Remember, this is just a sample of the details of meals we gave out during the 2014 campaign:

- In Iraq, we helped 800 families in the city of Najaf by giving food baskets containing rice, sugar, milk powder, tea leaves, cooking oil, lentils, eggs and dates. Many of those families had fled from ISIS in various northern cities such as Talafar, Sinjar and Mosul. Overall, 22 per cent of the population was living on less than US$2 a day.

- In Syria, 4,500 households were provided with bread packs to help ward off immediate hunger. The beneficiaries were internally displaced people from two villages in the Idlib suburbs, and the number of people who benefited was 22,500, with 240,000 meals delivered in total.

- In Lebanon, 220 families, a total of 1,320 people, benefited from the distribution of food packs. The beneficiaries were vulnerable families, specifically Syrian refugees living in the Saida, Ain al-Hilweh and Miyeh w Miyeh camps in South Lebanon. They were selected on the basis of the number of dependants, including young children and elderly family members, and women-headed households were given priority. In Pakistan, we gave food packs to 120 families from the Kashmiri refugee camps at Gulpur in the Kotli district and at Ambore in the Muzaffarabad district. People there were living in severe poverty, which meant food insecurity and the need to make dreadful choices – for example, between feeding a daughter or buying medicine for an ailing mother.

Wasim Akhar and Adeem at the Turkey-Syria border, delivering emergency aid, June 2015

"They were chronically poor, and living in tents and mud houses with no sources of income"

- In Afghanistan, 300 families in the Pul-e-Company IDP (internally displaced persons) camp in the 5th district of Kabul were provided with food parcels. These contained cooking oil, pulses, rice, green tea, dates and salt. The beneficiaries were families from Helmand, Uruzgan and Kandahar provinces. They were chronically poor, and living in tents and mud houses with no sources of income.

- In Bangladesh, where over 75 per cent of the population was living on less than US$2 a day, we gave out 253 food packs to beneficiaries living in poverty in disaster-prone, remote areas. The areas chosen were in the Rajbari and Dinajpur districts – hard-to-reach regions undergoing a severe food crisis.

- In Ethiopia, we gave 400 families in the Ginir district of the west Bale Zone (namely, Gamo Duksi and Gergeda) food packs containing wheat flour, rice and cooking oil. Distribution was carried out in collaboration with the elders of pastoralist rural peasant villages in areas where there were high levels of poverty, particularly in relation to food security. In total, 2,400 people were fed.

- In Sudan, 200 families in Khartoum were given food packs, with distribution taking place at a school. The packs contained sugar, dates, cooking oil, lentils and a local plant juice preferred by the beneficiaries. In total, 200 men, 200 women and 100 children were fed.

- In Somalia, 120 families totalling 720 people in IDP camps in the Hawle Wadag and Hodan districts of Mogadishu were given food packs containing rice, flour, sugar, dates, oil, tea and drinks. Although the need in the camps was so great that it went beyond the capacity of our feeding project, the Feed Our World offering covered these people's basic food needs for a month and a half, which itself was a remarkable achievement.

These are just a few of the stories from the 2014 Feed Our World campaign. Over the years that followed, the numbers have soared in each category and country in which we work, and even as I write they continue to climb. I think it's important to record these inaugural numbers, to see the human chain linking our irrepressible Team Orange volunteers and speakers on-air for seven and eleven days during our respective Guinness World Record fundraisers, and the people across thirty countries and regions so in need of help, who received it. That year alone, we worked in Afghanistan, Azerbaijan, Bangladesh, Djibouti, Eritrea, Ethiopia, The Gambia, Guinea, Guinea-Bissau, India, Iraq, Kashmir, Kenya, Lebanon, Mali, Mauritania, Nepal, Niger, Nigeria, Pakistan, Palestine, Rwanda, Senegal, Sierra Leone, Somalia, Sri Lanka, Sudan, Syria, Turkey and Yemen. Feed Our World had come of age.

Our other programmes were set up to operate in a similar way. During 2014, for example, we completed 20,640 *qurbanis*, which went on to feed thousands of people. Meat from the sacrificed animals was provided fresh to families or cooked by our teams at community Eid dinners for the needy. We worked in countries in both Africa and Asia, slaughtering sheep, cows, goats, camels and oxen to provide meat to families for whom, in many instances, this would be the only time of the year they could eat it. Imagine being so poor that you only have the option to eat meat once a year.

The OrphanKind programme benefited from the increased revenue, and through it we provided 9,413 sponsorships to children across Pakistan, Sudan, Bangladesh and Palestine. The Sheikh began to expand his partnership with ADD in The Gambia, and we opened more and more orphan homes there. Where we directly managed a home, we were guided by our experience of the original orphan homes (beginning with Mera Apna Ghar in Sohawa), rolling out a similar level of bespoke care, stringent safeguarding, protection and love across all the others. Where we worked with a partner such as ADD in The Gambia, we instructed them and expected them to follow the same standards and safeguarding provisions. The programme, as we had planned, offered orphan children a route out of poverty, and brighter futures. The plan was not just for them to be educated, but to become future leaders in their communities.

During Ramadan 2014, we launched the Hifz Orphan Programme as well. A *hafiz* or *hafiza* are the terms given, respectively, to a male or female who has committed to memory the entire Qur'an. A *hafiz* (the word means "guardian" as well as "one who memorises") is especially well respected by his community because of his ability to quote the entire Qur'an. For a family to have a *hafiz* among them is considered honourable. We decided, therefore, to launch this programme, through which orphans could be educated specifically on the teachings of the Qur'an. During its inaugural year, we created 2,717 such sponsorships.

Meanwhile, our Thirst Relief programme, created to provide clean, safe drinking water across twelve developing countries, really moved up a gear with the increase in revenue in 2014. A total of 1,974 wells were built. Each donor to Thirst Relief could choose to have a well built in their name, or in the name of a loved one, and we placed a plaque on each well to recognise the dedication. Our teams on the ground determined the most suitable locations for the wells, whether tube wells with hand pumps or deep wells with the traditional rope-and-bucket system, ensuring that as many people as possible benefited from a nearby source of clean water.

All these programmes – OrphanKind, Thirst Relief, Feed Our World, Qurbani, Hifz Orphan, Open Your Eyes – had been created by Rizwan and me to meet two primary objectives: they needed to fit the "Small Change, Big Difference" philosophy of requiring only minimal donations – in many cases, literally, pennies; and they needed to be scalable, so that as the revenues began to rise, we were able to increase the output exponentially, working with trusted partners on the ground. These programmes, and our vastly developed fundraising processes, provided the foundations for Penny Appeal for the years to come.

Feed Our World programme, Djibouti, East Africa 2019

At the same time, however, Penny Appeal – as a global charity aimed at helping the poor and needy – has always been ready to respond immediately to emergencies. Way back in 2010, we acted immediately when the earthquake occurred in Haiti, and raised funds that were then allocated to the charity Plan International. Now, during this transformative year of 2014–15, when we suddenly had so much more income to allocate, we were able to respond to a number of emergencies while still increasing our annual programme spend generously:

- An Ebola outbreak in West Africa, which began in March 2014, quickly reached epidemic proportions. Penny Appeal delivered aid to patients and people quarantined in homes in the Northern Province of Sierra Leone. Food packs, including staple items such as rice and oil, soap for washing and sweets were handed out in several towns and villages.

- Later that year, the fifty-day conflict in Gaza left thousands of families with no homes or livelihoods, and no reliable access to food, water or medical aid. It was a bleak situation that left children and adults fighting to survive. Our work in Gaza during this period was extensive, providing everything from family food packs to water tankers and medicine for entire medical centres. We provided a water tanker to supply clean water to schools and hospitals; 986 food packs; dozens of mobility aids, such as wheelchairs and walking sticks; an ambulance for emergency medical support and to transport patients to hospital; fifteen medical rooms, containing equipment such as beds, monitors and cabinets; a care centre for amputees and disabled and orphaned children, providing psychological support, education and training; an emergency section at Hayfa Charitable Medical Centre, comprising beds, monitors and other equipment; and additional emergency medical supplies.

- In 2014, we set up the first of our annual Winter Emergency campaigns, aiming to deal specifically with the problems caused by the winter weather. The programme worked across four countries, delivering life-saving items such as warm clothing (jumpers, shoes, coats, scarves, hats and gloves), nutritious food, hygiene products (soap, toothbrushes and toothpaste, sanitary towels) and sleeping items (blankets, mattresses and heaters) to people who had to endure snow, rain and ice during the season. In Gaza we provided 588 blankets, 500 jackets, 100 heaters and 320 bedding packs (blankets and mattresses); in Turkey, 12,000 Syrian refugees received warm clothing; in Lebanon, 116 families received blankets and warm clothing; and in Pakistan, 100 families received food packs, warm clothes and hygiene kits.

- In the spring of 2015, Nepal was struck by a devastating earthquake and subsequent large aftershocks. Over 9,000 people were killed, and some 23,000 injured. Entire villages were flattened, leaving hundreds of thousands of people homeless and without access to food, water and shelter. We mobilised teams immediately. Our work focused on two key areas: in open spaces where people were sleeping, we set up a hot-food cooking and distribution tent, ensuring that hundreds of people could get a nutritious meal; we also went to some remote villages to distribute food packs and household and hygiene items, helping those whose homes had been destroyed. In total, we provided 200 food packs, 200 essential family kits, 200 household packs and 10,500 cooked meals.

The methods we used in 2014–15 to allocate the sums raised during that year throughout the thirty countries and regions in which we now operated have remained consistent. Where we have skilled and trained people on the ground, such as in Pakistan, we can administer a substantial amount of aid ourselves, or commission works such as the building of a new orphan home. In other areas, such as Gaza, we wouldn't normally have Team Orange personnel in place. We therefore allocate donor funds to reliable partners such as Save the Children. What we don't do is build up our own staffing base unnecessarily; as many other charities have found, it is all too easy to swell the payroll and thereby diminish the funds available to give to the people who need them most. Our donors, predominantly charitable British Muslims, are always keen to see their funds being used in a practical way.

○

As Grandad told me, *you just keep going* – no matter what they throw at you. That's always been my way, and it's always been the Penny Appeal way. One gentleman who personified this way of thinking, at this exciting time in 2014–15, was Ahmad Bostan, who drove the Open Your Eyes campaign – which has continued to provide vital eyecare services in developing countries. He remains an inspiration to me. It was from him that I first heard the phrase: "Impossible spells *I'm Possible!*"

Ahmad is from Birmingham. He was born blind, and has overcome his disability with a strength and generosity of spirit that humbles me. He is now a Councillor at Birmingham City Council – the first blind person elected to such a position in his area. Motivated by a humanitarian spirit, he first began fundraising at the age of thirteen, when he volunteered on a local radio station called Unity FM. I recall contacting the station in 2009, asking them whether or not we could collaborate with them to raise funds for our Konsh Valley Educational Home. They suggested that I co-present a programme with Ahmad, then still in his teens. I met this seventeen-year-old lad and was impressed by his combination of high intelligence, eloquence and spiritual humility.

Ahmad was fundraising for a number of charities at the station then, but before long he became exclusively attached to Penny Appeal campaigns. He seemed from the start to understand the essence of the charity, the empathy with

"It was from Ahmad Bostan that I first heard the phrase: 'Impossible spells I'm Possible!'"

which we tried to operate.

Ahmad and I co-presented the programme on-air, and raised just over £10,000 in the space of a few hours for the Konsh Valley home. That airwave relationship with the people of Birmingham was built so strongly and passionately that, only two years later, we managed to raise over £275,000 in just sixteen hours at the height of the Gaza conflict. That shows you how comprehensively people there embraced the concept of "Small Change, Big Difference" – from the start.

Ahmad was, effectively, our first fundraiser. He is not only my dear friend, and an inspiration in the way he transcends his disability on a daily basis; he is also a crucial player in the whole Penny Appeal story. He always insisted that he had no need of payment for his services, and the most I could ever force upon him was the cost of taxi fare back home from the radio station – and even after a marathon twenty-four-hour stint of TV fundraising. He is now a trustee of Penny Appeal Pakistan, and is probably the most familiar face and voice of Penny Appeal to donors from his multiple appearances on our TV and radio fundraisers.

Ahmad really stepped up to the mark in 2012 when Rizwan and I developed our core strategy of long-term, sustainable campaigns. We asked Ahmad to be the radio voice of the first Feed Our World campaign during Ramadan 2012, and he worked brilliantly both with us and with the many volunteers who dropped everything to help us during that period. Then, in 2013, during our first live-television appeal on Ramadan TV, the three of us developed and matured some of the narratives we used on-air and on social media, and came up with a format that Ahmad delivered with unstinting passion and eloquence on television. Our donors responded immediately and favourably to his kind, informed presentations. As we began to have conversations about these projects, and to deliver more assistance in developing countries on the back of our campaigns, it was a natural development – with Ahmad now such a key member of the team – to begin to talk about sight, or lack thereof.

The issue of blindness in developing countries has been strikingly under-represented in the entire charity sector, both in 2012 and still today. There is simply not enough attention focused on the debilitating effects of damage to sight, or on the solutions that can be put into place to stop them. The issue is very much part of breaking the cycle of poverty we always talk about, and for Penny Appeal, addressing sight deprivation became a central programme objective. Blindness even in a single individual, like other disabilities, can have a negative impact on an entire family when you live in poverty; it can make the difference between having sufficient human resources to farm the land, and not.

The goal was to save people's sight. Our research showed that much blindness in the developing world is *preventable*. Extremes of weather – heat, cold, dust – can block the duct in the eyes that keeps them moist. Once those pores are blocked, the eyes go dry – and that's when sight begins to fail. Even a small donation can have a huge effect in enabling us to carry out examinations and provide remedies, so that eyesight is restored. In that sense, it's an unbelievably cheap task to prevent blindness, compared to a lot of other interventions. And the tasks can be as minimal as providing sunglasses for people working in the fields. Think about it: it's baking hot, the breeze is blowing tiny dust and grain particles into your face all day long as you bend over crops … it's no wonder people's eyesight is so easily affected. Implementing simple solutions – say, wearing the kind of sunglasses we might think nothing about picking up in Britain in preparation for a trip to the seaside – can have a drastic impact on daily living.

The mission-critical element is cash. Without it, you can't get started. You need a campaign. We called this one Open Your Eyes, with the dual meaning intended: we in the UK must open our own eyes to the needs of people in developing countries. If you can open your eyes, they can open theirs. We got the marketing right, went out to donors, brought the money in and were able to fund the programmes. We'd say to the programmes team: if we raised X amount of money, what could be done with it? They would research the particular developing region, work out what was needed and determine whether or not we could deliver the service or would need to bring in a third-party operator. We would then know how to break down the funding request to our donors: X amount will allow us to fund this number of eyesight programmes; but if we get Y, we can do that much more.

From the start, we were certain that we weren't going to do a blindness project just for the sake of it. It couldn't be tokenistic; it had to be real, comprehensive, and it had to deliver a level of service that we would expect to get back here in Britain. Even though Penny Appeal was still a young organisation with limited resources at its disposal, I insisted that service provision be as professional and compassionate as possible; we were never to compromise on any aspect of it.

Sohawa, near my family's village of Hathia Dhamial, had the first "eye camp". We went to the best eye hospital in the country, Shifa International in Islamabad, consulted with an eye surgeon there and told him what we wanted to do. He said, "OK, get me these people and these materials, we can do it next month". The redoubtable Habib Nawaz put together a project team that set up banners in Urdu telling villagers that the eye camp would be available at a certain time. Following the advice we had received in Islamabad, we gathered together one eye specialist and a couple of surgeons, plus a couple of nurses, and we kitted up a Suzuki van with donated glasses and eyedrops and other materials. We ran it like a military operation.

Ahmad and his father agreed to come out with us for that first eye camp in 2014, and it was a particularly memorable trip. I asked Ahmad to open this inaugural camp during that three-day visit: on the first day we went to see the Mera Apna Ghar orphan home and spent some time with the children; on the second day, we went to build some water wells; and on the third day, we held the first Open Your Eyes camp. Over 400 people attended; many queued up overnight. People of all ages, from babies through to grandparents, came, often walking over very difficult terrain to get there – and there had been thunderstorms and rain the previous day. There was some anxiety in the queue, as people at the back worried that they wouldn't be seen to. Apparently, previous field eye clinics in Pakistan had closed after they met their quota; often, people wouldn't be seen by a specialist or even a nurse. We were determined that even if we had to stay there all night, we would make sure that every person would be examined and given the treatment they needed.

Again, that goes back to Penny Appeal's original vision, refusing to do anything half-heartedly. We know that when we say we are going to deliver a project, we deliver it properly. You've got to believe in it, pledge to it, if you really want to make a difference. This attitude goes to the very heart of the organisation itself, and, actually, harks back to the Islamic principles on which it is based, and the famous *Hadith* in which the Holy Prophet, Peace Be Upon Him, says: "None of you can be true Muslims unless you love for your brother what you love for yourself." "Brother" here means your fellow human being – basically, everyone. Sadly, that is not the approach of many organisations. But at Penny Appeal, we never believed there was anything we could *not* do for people, if we put our minds to it: Impossible spells *I'm possible*!

Once the camp opened, it was run with great efficiency. One person would have their eyes checked; if the surgeon confirmed that a minor operation was needed, that person would go over to another queue, have their eyes cleaned and ready to be treated. Then there'd be another queue with people being fitted for glasses, and another for people having tests. All the time the nurses went around keeping everything clean, reassuring the elderly and the fearful. Because healthcare is so rare in some of these remote rural areas, many people benefit simply from basic things such as hygiene instruction, eyedrops and so on. A minority would need some kind of surgery, and most of the minor operations could be carried out at the camp itself. If anyone needed major treatment, we got them to the specialist hospital in Islamabad, where they would stay in overnight.

It was fascinating to watch Ahmad respond to this new environment. He is a remarkably self-reliant fellow: back in the UK, he will get himself from Birmingham to our offices in Wakefield with no assistance. But out in rural Pakistan, he had to be guided all the way, because just one stumble out there can mean falling down a slope or toppling into an open sewer; it was hard enough for a fully sighted person not to take a knock and fall down on the rocky hills. I could see him registering the difference in the daily challenges that blind and visually impaired people faced out there. I asked him recently how much of an impact that had on him, and he replied:

The people in that first eye camp were very curious about me, how I lived my life as a blind person in the UK. I felt embarrassed, actually, because of how much I have and how little they had. It really humbled me. Even the most basic adaptations in my life, like having a Braille computer so I can write and communicate – this would be such a significant thing for them. In the UK, the equipment that blind and visually impaired people use costs thousands of pounds, and we have charities and organisations set up specifically just to fund that kind of equipment. Obviously, that kind of equipment is completely beyond the reach of someone in Pakistan. So the people in the camp were taken aback by the facilities I had, and I was equally taken aback by the poverty and disability with which they had to live their daily lives.

That experience has been replicated by others in our organisation; as soon as someone sees or hears of issues in a developing country that we might be able to help with, then the next task is to get back to the UK to fundraise the money in order to tackle it. Just seeing those aspects of poverty in real life, it really brings home to you the urgency of responding with the right charity. People with disabilities in developing countries are prisoners in their own home. They can't go out because the terrain is far too difficult. I'm very independent here in the UK, but in Pakistan, because of the terrain, I had to be guided throughout. And that is the everyday reality for people with impaired vision there.

A lot of people living with disabilities there become dehumanised, their conditions are so severe. It's a daily process of loneliness, depression and ultimately, sadly, often suicidal thoughts.

When Habib and I discussed how to set up that first camp, we had to think properly about the environment. Is it the wet season or the dry season? Are the days long and hot? Will people need food and drink while they're waiting? How long will it take people to get to the camp? What will the facilities be like if they need to stay overnight?

We've always had full support from local people, who offer us land to use and open up their facilities to us, because they know that we're helping the community – youngsters, the elderly. They know that people won't have to save up for months or even years to be able to go to a local hospital to get treated. They know they're going to get the best treatment here, for free.

For us, setting up an eye camp is a relatively minor and cost-effective process. And while most of us can get free care on the NHS, the difference in the lives of not only the individual concerned but their families, too, is huge. Unfortunately, there is a great deal of stigma around disability in many developing countries; when you're living in poverty, disability is just another burden. For example, somebody in the house won't be able to go to work and earn money, because they must stay at home and look after the daughter, or father, or grandmother who's got a disability. It's easy for us to say, "How terrible, how can you consider that a burden, surely you would do that just because they're family!" But that is the perspective of Western privilege. You begin to understand that there is an entirely different perspective to disability when you live in poverty. These are not easy decisions, and families can't make them without sacrificing something else.

That first trip in 2014 profoundly affected how we've done things since, and how we've managed the Open Your Eyes campaign. Just as important as the medical procedures we deliver is the act of care itself. Open Your Eyes teams in the developing countries in which we're working are responsible for every element connected with the provision of service. For example, if you have suffered for years from visual impairment and then get your sight back, that recovery in itself can become a new burden requiring support to deal with: now you can see again, you've got to get back into the daily processes of managing livestock, ploughing fields and so on. That level of holistic care makes Open Your Eyes, and Penny Appeal as a whole, different from most other charities. There is a genuine,

"There was pin-drop silence in the whole room whilst we all stood, helpless in the face of their future in darkness."

personal commitment to everything we do in this organisation.

On the eye-camp trip, I think we were all affected by one incident in particular. An old, blind man had brought his seventeen-year-old grandson, who was blind too. The old man said, "I don't need my eyes fixed; I've had my life. But my grandson ... please save my grandson's eyes."

Hassan, the grandson, came before the doctor and said: "Thank you, thank you, I haven't been able to see for a year now." He broke down in tears and added: "Doctor Sahib, you are my only hope. Please, please help me."

Doctor Youssef, the ophthalmologist that day, examined the boy's eyes and soon became despondent. Afterwards, he said to us: "If I'd only seen Hassan six weeks earlier, I could have saved his sight." Hassan's sight had gone because of his unhygienic living environment, Doctor Youssef told us.

We asked Hassan, "Do you go to school? Do you have special facilities?" But he had nothing at all, it appeared. This young man was deprived of a normal life because his family was simply too poor to provide him with any help. I thought to myself: for his mother and father to hear that six weeks earlier, if they'd had the money and the facilities, this lad's sight could have been saved ... that would be heart-breaking. Both Hassan and his grandfather wept upon hearing this from Doctor Youssef. There was pin-drop silence in the whole room whilst we all stood, helpless in the face of their future in darkness, without support to cope.

I know that Ahmad was truly shocked by the level of poverty and deprivation he witnessed on that trip. To actually experience first-hand the problems that blind and visually impaired people there had to contend with every day of their lives really brought home to all of us how fortunate we are – and also how much more work we have to do. We had to send Hassan back to his family, where he would have continued – blind though he was – to act as the main carer for his grandfather while his parents worked in the fields. To this day, I think of him, and of those lost six weeks.

Open Your Eyes is a perfect example of how Penny Appeal works, taking small change and making a big difference with it, using pennies to make major improvements for individuals and families in developing countries. Today there are 285 million people in the world who are visually impaired, and 90 per cent of them live in the developing world. Of those visual impairments, 80 per cent are preventable – and many can be cured. For some people, a short and simple eye examination is enough to make a life-changing difference, preventing their vision from deteriorating into blindness. We always work with the best partners in each country, whether that's lining up with a hospital such as the one in Islamabad or working with a registered charity providing eyecare relief.

Just over a year ago, we worked with the Friends of the Blind Association in Palestine to promote the educational rights of sixty-five impoverished Palestinian children, who are either blind or have very poor eyesight. We paid the children's tuition fees for 2019, provided a Braille version of the Palestinian curriculum, secured accommodation for the ones living in remote West Bank villages and cities and provided for stationery, food, school uniforms, medicine and transportation. We used the same holistic, comprehensive approach that Ahmad talked about, looking at the issues around the visual impairment that made family life so difficult.

Thus, Open your Eyes opens the door to opportunity, ensuring that nobody is left in the dark. For as little as 16p per day from a UK donor, we are able to start making a difference to someone's failing eyesight somewhere in the world. Over the next ten years, and over the ten years after that, I want thousands and thousands of multiples of those 16p to keep making real changes through the Open Your Eyes appeal.

When people say something is "impossible", I always think of Ahmad Bostan on that trip to Sohawa in 2014, constantly trying to get about on the uneven land without needing to ask for assistance, tripping up over stones, falling in a ditch – but always getting up with that wry smile on his face. He brought some hope to people that day, and he continues to do so seven years later.

CHAPTER NINE

ON THE ROAD

There has been an easy, natural feel to the way Penny Appeal has accommodated such an explosive rate of growth, and I put that down to two things: our attitude – we have never been stuffy or formal, and have always retained our roots with our donor community; and our authenticity – we have always prioritised delivery of programmes as promised, anywhere in the world. Sometimes our refusal to invest in procedures over programmes has done us a disservice, but I still hold that our ability to put food into the mouths of deserving hungry people overrules all such concerns.

We are, first and foremost, a donor-led organisation. We rely on our donors to support both our regular programmes and emergency appeals, and we encourage them to spread the word amongst their friends and family. We want the community to feel that we are accessible, friendly, and completely responsive to those we help. Our success is a huge blessing from God, we believe, for service to His people. By trusting in the instincts of our donors, we know that we shall be able to fulfil their wishes all over the world.

Our great step forward into television fundraising in 2014 enabled us to open up conversations with British Muslims who, back then, were not savvy digital types. We gained access to all the aunties and uncles who were catching up on their Bollywood and Lollywood dramas and their news updates, and we gave them a sense of participation, the sense that their donations were being handled visibly. We were the opposite of the many old-world traditional charity institutes.

But there was one more step to go for us to truly become one with our community of British Muslims. While television was an excellent means of communication with our core donating audience, the donor is still in his or her living room, watching a flickering screen. I was talking about this after our record-breaking television event in 2014 with the actor, presenter, fundraiser and all-round good guy Rahim Jung.

"You've made a breakthrough, Adeem, well done," he said. I thanked him, told him how it had been such a strong team effort and thanked him for his part in the journey and his support. "It's good," he continued. "Now, for the first time, the Muslim charity sector knows who you are. You've arrived."

I was waiting for the "but".

"But," he said, "the mainstream Muslim donors still don't really know you. They've seen the orange logo on TV now. They've heard Rizwan Khaliq making an appeal, they've heard Jawad Sarwar making an appeal, they've heard Sister Aala making an appeal. And they've responded to that, responded amazingly with what I've seen. But they still don't *know* you like you know the people in your street, the people at your mosque. They haven't met your team face-to-face, Adeem. Penny Appeal, it needs to get out and meet its donors."

Immediately, I knew he was right. I was an entrepreneur; I'd built up a successful Internet business without using TV at all. What we *had* done was to spread the word from person to person, slowly and methodically, on foot. We'd turned up outside mosques and chicken shops and taxi stands with leaflets advertising Single Muslim. We'd staged speed-dating events for Muslims – to meet prospective partners, but mostly to spread the word that there was now an online service available to Muslims specifically for that purpose. Once you are physically amongst other people, you both become more real to them, and you become more trusted. It's a marketing way of saying, "here I am, you can trust me". Experienced marketeers learn that you can't remain isolated; you need to go to where your audience is.

Rahim was spot-on: this was going to be the next stage in Penny Appeal's growth. I went back to the Penny Appeal office the day after the Guinness World Record TV appeal.

"Guys, we need Penny Appeal to go on the road. We need to get out and meet people."

"But Adeem," the team members said. "None of us has ever put on an event. We don't know how to do it."

"Don't worry," I replied. "We need to find something we can take out on the road for two or three months, something that will appeal to our donors, help us spread the message about Penny Appeal and ultimately help us to raise funds. Once we've found that something, the rest will be easy."

The days and nights my Single Muslim team and I had put in years before, perfecting the running of our dating nights at venues around the country, were invaluable as I began to coach the Penny Appeal guys on how to stage events. We had learned so much in those early days: what kind of venue worked best; the attendance numbers you needed for the most effective evening; how long in advance you should begin to market tickets, and at what price point; how to factor in elements such as bad weather on the night; how to remain in contact afterwards with the attendees. My Single Muslim team had perfected all this, and now once again I was able to transfer the knowledge to Penny Appeal.

Soon after we'd taken the decision to move into events, a friend of mine told me about an American comedian called Omar Regan. Omar apparently was trying to crowdfund a movie called *American Sharia*, which wanted to present a more positive image of Islam via Hollywood to the Western world. I liked the idea. I enjoyed American movies, and I liked the idea of someone wanting to take a positive approach to counter negative stereotypes about Islam. I researched Omar, and hunted down his number to give him a call.

SMALL CHANGE, BIG DIFFERENCE
SMALL CHANGE, BIG DIFFERENCE

Let me tell you, you haven't really experienced all that life has to offer until you've had a phone call with Omar Regan. The man is a pressure cooker of energy, jokes, intelligence, sincerity, generosity and creativity. Ideas and fantasies fire out of him like a Catherine wheel. He grew up in Detroit but moved to Los Angeles when he was nineteen to pursue a career in stand-up. He spent years scratching out a living and pursuing his dream while caring for his kids in a one-bed Hollywood apartment. He worked as a body double for Chris Tucker in the Hollywood blockbuster *Rush Hour 2*. He has known adversity, and he has overcome it.

As with many of the comedians we came to work with at our live events over the coming years, Omar wasn't a household name when I first met him. But he and I clicked on our first phone call, and I made a personal contribution to his crowdfunded movie. I liked him and trusted him; he made me laugh, and I admired the serious intent behind the laughter to promote greater integration of Muslims and people of other faiths. I loved the idea of the movie, of bringing people together with comedy to present a positive view of our community and of Islam. I had a feeling we could work together. Before we ended the call, and without really having a plan in place, I asked him to come to Wakefield for a meeting.

Omar had never been to Wakefield. To this day, he keeps telling me how cold it was, that winter of 2014. But despite shivering under as many layers of sweaters and Team Orange hoodies as we could get on him, he brought our Penny Appeal building to light for two days. My colleagues loved him, and he seemed to love us back. He is genuinely fierce in his commitment to Muslim charity, and he loved the energy of our mostly young team. After two days of talks, we'd come to an agreement: we would provide him with the financial support to complete *American Sharia*, and in return we'd get UK rights to tour the film for Penny Appeal. I drove him back to Manchester Airport, shook his hand and told him I looked forward to him coming back in February 2015 with the finished film. My team had already started researching venues for the nationwide tour.

We got on with what we needed to do, booking the famous Hackney Empire in East London for the opening show on 11 February. Then we booked dates at venues in Birmingham, Bolton, Bradford, Bristol, Cardiff, Coventry, Derby, Edinburgh, Glasgow, Leeds, Leicester, Liverpool, Luton, Manchester, Middlesbrough, Newcastle, Nottingham, Sheffield and Slough. We would have matinée shows, doubling up in the large cities, a non-stop twenty-two locations in one month. I started planning how we could run each evening with a dedicated fundraiser targeted at our current programmes. As we started to market the tour, the first ticket sales came in. We had an agreement with Omar to stage payments to him to complete the film as sales began to flow.

I phoned Omar in Los Angeles. "How's our film going, Omar?"

"We've got a problem."

"What problem?"

"The problem is, *Batman*'s come to town."

"I don't care where Batman is, Omar, where's our film?"

He explained that when Hollywood starts working on a big film, all the key personnel such as editors and sound engineers get hoovered up by this enormous blockbuster machine. He said he hadn't been able to finish the film yet.

We carried on with our preparations and marketing. Rahim agreed to work with us on the tour as the key fundraiser, making a presentation to the audience halfway through the film. We'd set the ticket price at £5, which was pretty standard in 2015 for charity events in the UK and enabled us to market the film to everyone, rather than making it an exclusive evening. This was Omar's first film, so we made sure our audience realised in advance that although this was going to be a great experience, they weren't necessarily going to be watching *Gone with the Wind*. This was, we promised, going to be a fun British Muslim family evening, with the opportunity to have a look at the first cut of a terrific American comedian's first film, and to hear news about Penny Appeal's work overseas and participate in fundraising for orphan homes and feeding the homeless. We were developing our new live-event process on the hoof, organically, and it felt like it was working.

I phoned Omar again a couple of weeks later.

"Yeah, yeah, Adeem, it's all cool. We're doing really well. No worries."

But it turned out his film team had disappeared, and he was having issues trying to find them.

"Can we see something soon, Omar?"

"Yeah, yeah, nearly there … not long!"

By now, we'd put the trailer for *American Sharia* out across the UK, and were selling tickets. The whole Muslim community in the UK was getting excited about this new Muslim movie filmed in Hollywood. We'd hired the venues, hired a million-amp projector that came in a cage, with its own security van. I'd booked five celebrities to join us on the tour, and we'd arranged hotel rooms and transport for them.

I got back on the phone to Omar. "Omar, my friend," I said. "I'm starting to get a bit uncomfortable. When are we going to see the film?"

"Don't worry, don't worry! I've got a new team on it. We're going to be fine!"

"Omar," I said. "I *am* worried. I'm coming to America."

I booked a flight to Los Angeles. Omar met me at the airport. He's the loveliest, most hospitable man. He showed me to the best restaurants in town, guided me down Hollywood

Boulevard and to all the famous movie landmarks. From his apartment, we could see the famous HOLLYWOOD sign. I couldn't have had a funnier, more generous, more charming host.

After two days, though, I still hadn't seen the movie.

"Omar," I said on the second evening, "can I see the movie?"

"Breakfast time, Adeem. We'll watch the movie tomorrow at breakfast."

So we did. We watched the movie over a full American breakfast at Lilly's Café in downtown Hollywood, and, while it contained all of Omar's brilliance and humour and spirit, it still wasn't finished: the sound editing wasn't done; the colour grading wasn't done. It was a great film; it just didn't yet have the polish he'd hoped it would have by now. It wasn't ready, and we had the Hackney Empire waiting for us.

Adeem with Omar Regan in California, 2015

Never mind. We'd explained to our audience that this was a work in progress. And when Omar flew over with the still-not-quite-complete film, the audiences in Hackney, Birmingham, Newcastle ... loved it! They loved Omar and his passion, loved his humour and his take on tackling Hollywood's unfair perspectives on our faith. And he loved being with the audiences, finding out which elements worked best, which needed improving. He took notes every night in his notebook. As we toured the film around Britain, Omar was editing the film as he went.

I learned a lot from Omar through that tour. He was dedicated, always smiling no matter how difficult something was. His smile was infectious, and his energy was the charger for everyone's long days and endless traveling up and down the country. He fitted right into the Penny Appeal's can-do, 'never give up' culture. To this day, Omar is very much Team Orange.

○

The whole experience was so very Penny Appeal. At its heart lay a lot of trust, which both Omar and our dedicated Team Orange volunteers and fundraisers rewarded many times over. Even now, five years on, people come up to me and tell me what a great evening out they'd had going to see the first showing of *American Sharia* in the UK. (It's available today on Amazon Prime, too.) Even five years later, Penny Appeal still receives £200,000 every year from charitable direct debits set up during the *American Sharia* campaign. Now that's what you call a fundraising legacy!

It is difficult to underestimate just how significant this tour was: until then, the idea of a Muslim entertainment tour in the UK was virtually unknown. Muslims might go out to see a star like Ed Sheeran play in Manchester; non-Muslims might go see a show by Yusuf/Cat Stevens; but the idea of an expressly

"British Muslims are British as well as Muslim, and love nothing more than to be amongst friends and family in a safe, positive environment."

Muslim film, created by an artist like Omar to show the faith in a positive way, becoming the focus of a family evening out across the country ... this was pretty much unheard of. There is still a strongly conservative element within our community that, while not expressly opposed to public entertainment, shies away from it. But British Muslims are British as well as Muslim, and love nothing more than to be amongst friends and family in a safe, positive environment. With the *American Sharia* tour, we provided that. Omar had written and directed a film that scrupulously avoided non-family-friendly elements such as swearing and nudity; the venues we chose were friendly as well; the price of the ticket was accessible to all; and the Team Orange volunteers and fundraisers were positive and dynamic when they spoke about the charitable projects around the world that the evening would support.

Penny Appeal doesn't just raise funds for the poor. It is also a very visible emblem of integration for British Muslims, a route for us to show how proud we are of both our faith and the country in which we live. As I sat at the back of the auditorium at each of the shows, I recognised the truth of what Rahim Jung had said the year before: even with a great digital presence and TV appeals, we still hadn't really embraced our own community. Now, as I watched mums and dads, aunties and uncles, boys and girls laughing until the tears rolled down their cheeks as Omar's character – a blundering LA Muslim cop named Mohammed – delivered his lines, I saw that this was where Penny Appeal needed to live: right there, amongst its donor community. Charity is so fundamental to our faith, to our identities, and here we had an event where giving could sit alongside fun and family; it was a joy. As well as raising money for worthy causes, we were, all of us, in those cinemas, carving out a modern British Muslim identity – and I felt humbled to be part of it.

The Penny Appeal team, like they always do, got their heads around the mechanics of live events very quickly once I'd mentored them. I'd discovered myself several years earlier that there were some pretty hard and fast rules to selling live-event tickets successfully – the kinds of rules that music promoters such as Harvey Goldsmith learned decades ago. First, you needed to work out your breakeven point, where your ticket sales would cover the cost of the show; the timeline; and the 'runway' to each show. Then you needed to decide how you would profile the show in ticket marketing. Soon we were learning all the tricks of the trade, such as releasing blocs of tickets in stages, so that each bloc had to sell out before more went on sale. We even realised that you could oversell an event by up to 10 per cent, because for every event there would always be that number of no-shows: people who either forgot they had ordered, even after email and SMS reminders, or had something more pressing to do that evening. Again, all the lessons we had learned when hosting Single Muslim dating events were now being enjoyed by Penny Appeal. We didn't have to hire consultants or pay expensive producers; I was able to pass on the fruits of my own commercial experience, and we did it all ourselves.

The most important thing we learned was about audience

numbers. Remember, if one unexpected outcome had been this great sense of community integration, our primary objective was always to raise money for our charity programmes. On the *American Sharia* tour, we would have Omar open the evening, let the audience get to know him and enjoy his rapid-fire, quick-thinking wit; then we'd play the first half of the film. During the intermission, Rahim Jung or one of our other regular fundraisers would come onstage and hold a thirty-minute fundraiser presentation. (Rahim's performance every night was something to behold.)

The audience was already in good humour by then. They were on a rare evening out with family, and they'd just been rocking in their seats with laughter at the first half of Omar's movie.

Rahim would stand up to address them: "Tonight, here in Birmingham, we're going to build an orphan home in West Africa. An orphan home costs £40,000. Who's got £40,000? No? Are there two people with £20,000? Are there four people with £10,000?" (You'd be surprised: every now and then, some generous soul would put their hand up to offer the full £40,000!) Rahim's eloquent, respectfully delivered patter would have Team Orange volunteers running around the audience picking up pledges as donors offered £5,000, £50, £500 ... whatever they wanted to contribute. By the end of the session, Rahim would announce, to huge applause: "Ladies and gentlemen, brothers and sisters, tonight we have built *three* orphan homes. That's three homes where children with no parents can thrive, get an education, learn to read, grow into adults. We've done that, tonight. Thanks to all those who donated, and thanks to everyone else for your patience in allowing us to raise funds to help the needy."

We worked out that the perfect number for a live fundraising event like this was between 350–450 people. The charity sector had established, long before us, a very low entry point for tickets. We were selling tickets for the night at just £5, because that's what people expected to pay. So we couldn't raise huge amounts from the ticket sales, and in any case we had already committed the bulk of that to funding Omar's completion of the film, renting the projector and so on. Therefore, the fundraising element was crucial. And what we discovered was that more than 450 people was actually *too many* people in the room for Rahim to be able to reach them all; some people would be raising their hands at the back, and he wouldn't see them; with a thousand people in the audience, the Team Orange volunteers couldn't get around easily enough. But if you had fewer than 350 people, then you couldn't raise enough money to make the whole evening worthwhile.

It worked. On that first twenty-two-city tour, Penny Appeal raised over £1 million, the great bulk of which, after we had paid for the costs of the tour, went to our programmes in developing countries. Over 10,000 people saw the film on that tour. We were getting about five times return on our investment, meaning that our programmes would benefit significantly from this new venture into the live-entertainment world. Until the hiccup caused by the Covid-19 pandemic of 2020, live events remained a core element of our fundraising and community engagement process – about 20 per cent of our annual income.

My "Universal Adaptor", Yousaf Razaq, the powerful fundraising director from Bradford, had been telling me for some time that Penny Appeal should hook up with internationally acclaimed British Muslim singer-songwriter Sami Yusuf. Straight after the *American Sharia* tour, we were able to coordinate with Sami on an eight-city UK tour. With tickets selling at a very affordable £10, we were able to energise our donor base once more and bring families out for a night of extraordinary music. The evening's show began with a warm-up from the now-famous *Britain's Got Talent* finalist of 2020, Nabil Abdul Rashid, followed by another highly effective fundraiser – this time specifically for OrphanKind, and conducted with great professionalism and spirit by broadcaster and Imam Ajmal Masroor. After the fundraiser, Sami would come back on to play a storming set, and our donors would leave feeling like they had been part of a very special night – which, in fact, we all had been. Over the nine nights of the tour, we raised half a million pounds in support of our orphan sponsorships and homes.

I applied the same financial rigour to our live events as I would have done for my commercial business. At Single Muslim, we needed to get a return on investment of at least four times if we were to carry on, for example, advertising through Google or Facebook. As soon as it dropped below that, we would cut the advertising. This simple equation meant that it didn't matter if our investment was £1,000 or £10,000 or £100,000 – as long as we were getting back four times the amount, it was worth it. In the same way, as long as events for Penny Appeal brought us back at least four times the amount they cost us to stage, they could continue. We had to be hard-headed as well as community-minded: no matter how much our community enjoyed the events, and no matter how much we enjoyed engaging with it in turn, we always had to prove that the events delivered that kind of revenue to our overseas programmes. At the end of the day, the only superstars we were trying to have an impact on were the people to whom our audiences were donating – the beneficiaries of all this effort. They were the most important people in all this razzamatazz. It was always all about the recipients.

Ramy Youssef, winner of the Golden Globe Award for Best
Actor – Comedy, on tour with Penny Appeal, 2017

We expanded our live-events repertoire further in the autumn of 2015, taking a group of brilliant Muslim stand-up comedians on a twelve-city tour of the UK. Borrowing from the name of our friend Omar Regan's production company – Halalywood – we set out to create a "halal-arious" comedy tour of Britain. The Super Muslim Comedy Tour featured Omar himself on a welcome second visit to be with us that year, together with Baba Ali, Moses the Comic, Nabil Abdul Rashid, Shaista Aziz, Sheraz Yousaf, Prince Abdi, Abdullah Afzal and Jeff Mirza. Many of the Muslim comedians on this tour, and on future ones, were at the early stages of their careers when they joined Penny Appeal, and the faith we placed in them was rewarded in typical Team Orange style, with knockout performances and future glory in their stand-up careers.

We applied the same discipline as before: strong pre-event marketing to our donor base, accessibly priced tickets, excellent work from the comedians interwoven with professionally run fundraisers for our campaigns. Once more, we were successful: over £500,000 was raised to help both refugees and orphans. Just this twelve-city tour alone meant that 4,776 refugee families could be helped in several different countries with food, hygiene items, sleeping bags and shelter. And 474 orphan sponsorships were created, giving vulnerable children loving and secure homes.

The Super Muslim Comedy Tour returned, bigger and better, the following year, with a starry line-up: Omar Regan, Preacher Moss, Azhar Usman, Abdullah Afzal, Prince Abdi, Moses The Comic, Ramy Youssef, Kae Kurd, Omar Hamdi and Mistah Islah. We toured Slough, London, Bolton, Nottingham, Birmingham, Coventry, Blackburn, Leicester, Sheffield, Bradford, Newcastle and Manchester.

While we would never claim to have invented the idea of the Muslim comedy tour, I think it's fair to say that our unique take on the genre brought it into the grassroots communities like never before and removed what had, until then, been a sense that 'Muslim comedy' was more of a niche arts concept. In the US, for example, Muslim comedy and comedians had been established for some time, but in the UK, it wasn't really until we took our tours out on the road that Muslim comedy began to appear more mainstream. By insisting that the nights be financially accessible, we made it possible for an entire family to attend together, and having people come out to see comedy for the first time in their lives was a real achievement in many ways. It wasn't just that we were able to be amongst our community in a real, live environment, but also that Penny Appeal was representative of a new kind of integrated, confident British Muslim life that could allow young and old to express themselves: unapologetically Muslim and unmistakably British. Only with such freedom can we build futures for our younger generations, give them the sense of possibility, of hope. I feel very passionately that these supposedly secondary outcomes of events such as the Super Muslim Comedy Tour have been significant for the broader notions of freedom and opportunity in our country.

There was also a further outcome that became more and more intentional as the years went by. Right from the start, our events went down a treat with Muslim audiences. Year on year we would bring exhilarating and inspiring events to Muslim communities, from spiritually infused film tours to pantomime shows for the kids. Given the relatively recent presence of Muslims in the UK as a community, we lack schemes that encourage them into creative spaces. Most parents have very immediate financial concerns, so non-traditional careers are seldom encouraged by the older generations. This means that, sadly, we don't nurture talented young people from within our community, especially creative ones. This, in turn, means

Penny Appeal has provided aid to 49 million beneficiaries since its founding in 2009

Coronavirus Emergency – 157,260 PPE distributed, 15,615 food packs for those in need, 31,460 health/hygiene packs

Qurbani – 29,562,295 Qurbani meals served, 89,855 Qurbanis performed

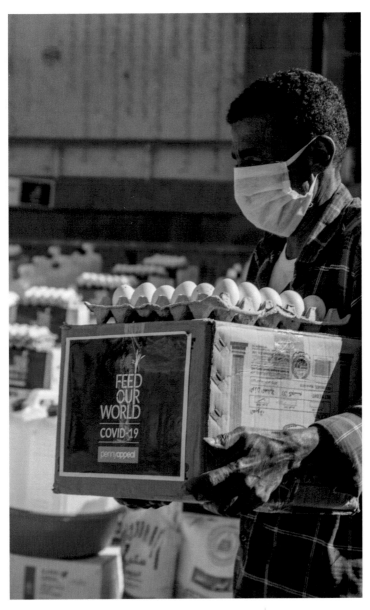

Feed Our World – 47 countries reached, 160,120 beneficiaries estimated, 1,517,070 meals served in past year, 50,569 meals served each day (Average, based on Ramadan 2020)

Adopt a Gran – 5 countries reached, 9,672 Adopt a Gran sponsorships

Open Your Eyes – 4 countries reached, 1,190 sight-saving operations

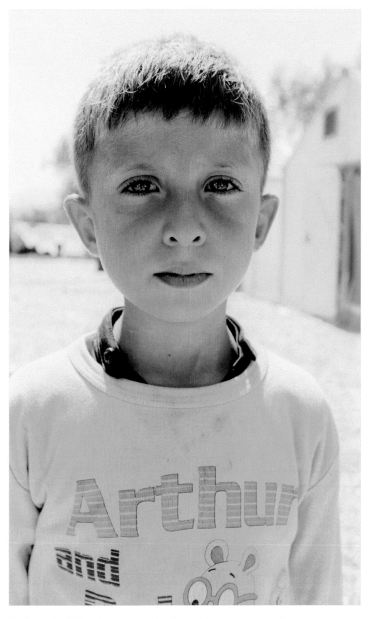

Orphans – 90,923 orphan sponsorships, 9 countries reached, 58,958 OrphanKind sponsorships, 31,965 Hifz Orphan sponsorships

Penny Appeal at Home – 150,270 hot meals served in the UK, 18 cities reached, 14,502 helpline calls answered, Helpline has been open for 14,196 hours, 1,800 counselling sessions, 16,534 COVID-19 UK beneficiaries

"Penny Appeal had finally found its identity as the People's Charity."

that the best-case scenario for these talented Muslims is to find spaces outside the community to nurture their creativity and craft, and maybe – just maybe – they return to Muslim spaces and contribute back. More often than not, though, it means that creative spark just withers away instead. With Penny Appeal, we had a chance to do something about it. Our events fast became springboards for emerging Muslim talent. Now, by no stretch of the imagination would I say we produced these stars, but in recent years so many talented Muslims who have cut their teeth working with charities just like our own have made it in the mainstream. I'm immensely proud that we were one of the first organisations ever to host the incredible comedian and actor Guz Khan, for example, who has gone on to star in Hollywood films and to have his own BBC comedy-drama series. Likewise, *Britain's Got Talent* finalist Nabil Abdul Rashid; Channel 4's Tez Ilyas; and so many more. In fact, in 2017, we launched "The Big Muslim Variety Show", for which we searched for performers looking to reach wider audiences, and giving a platform to next-generation creatives who, in turn, inspire our Muslim audiences, all the while raising funds for lifesaving campaigns. We've toured films, hosted comedians from every walk of life, put on plays and brought over singers, rappers and poets from all over the world. We've had beatboxers, musicians, actors, even breakdancers. We did our best to ensure that the talents we hosted were extended every professional courtesy, paid fairly and made to feel part of Team Orange.

Penny Appeal, is, after all, a British charity. We are not linked in any way, formally or informally, with a specific branch of Islam, or with a specific spiritual leader or organisation. We represent the *Muslim community of Britain*, and we engage with and rely upon that community in so many different ways. It is our root, and this close connection enables us to collaborate at ground level in ways that other charities just can't. We can work alongside non-Muslim British associates and audiences as well, because we share the same national way of life. That's the DNA of Penny Appeal: we're British Muslims and we want to do good stuff. To do that, and to make a big difference, we can only rely on British donors giving us their small change.

Going on the road in 2015 was the final piece in the jigsaw for me: this completed the picture of how I imagined Penny Appeal to be. By providing us with a permanent anchor in our community, it enabled us to have confidence in our ability to fulfil our programme commitments. I knew then, in 2015, that we would be able to start delivering more meals through Feed Our World, open more orphan homes through OrphanKind, fix more eyes through Open Your Eyes, build more clean water wells through Thirst Relief – because we had now physically established ourselves amongst the people of our community, and allowed them to embrace us. For the donors' faith in us is our only legitimacy. I believe that most British donors fundamentally want the same thing that I want: to be of assistance to those less fortunate than themselves. That's it; it's no more complicated than that. Most of them don't want to get caught up in politics or sectarian disagreements or opposing allegiances to different spiritual leaders. They lead the same busy lives that I do; they have children of their own to feed and care for, and the pressures of work and the demands of an ever more technologically connected world. With so much going on already, they want to have faith in a charity that represents the way they live their lives, and to believe that charity will stand alongside them in their desire to assist the unfortunate.

Penny Appeal had finally found its identity as the People's Charity. We were never going to be like the other, more traditional Muslim charities, which are all linked one way or another to this group or that group, to long lines of inheritance, fathers passing down traditions to sons. As someone who lost that inheritance line with the death of his own father, I was never going to have an instinct to follow a particular path within our faith, and when I created the charity, I was never going to align us to one particular mosque or spiritual leader or group. Instead, I had the example of my mum, who did so much to integrate herself and us into the local community in Wakefield, whose bustling, energetic, entrepreneurial behaviour inspired me in ways I would never have been, without her.

Mum was always the most open-minded of people. Women of different races, colours and faiths were regulars at our house when I was growing up. Mum always supported people no matter where they came from or what they believed in. I know that the open-mindedness that has always characterised Penny Appeal, particularly its recruitment policy, came from Mum's example. Her spirit shaped me and in turn shaped Penny Appeal's policy of celebrating difference, honouring diversity and inclusion and always keeping our doors open to everyone, regardless of who is knocking.

CHAPTER TEN

CHARITY BEGINS AT HOME

The figures said it all: in the year ending April 2015, Penny Appeal had a total income of just under £9 million. In the year ending April 2016, that leaped to almost £14 million; then, twelve months later, by April 2017, it had climbed to almost £19 million. By this stage, we were now able to spend significantly more on our projects in developing countries: £4 million on emergency relief, £2.2 million on food parcels, £1 million on building wells and other water projects and so forth. Compared to what we had been able to spend just three years earlier, we were now in a position to make substantial improvements to the lives of millions. We were beginning to have the capacity to intervene noticeably in the cycles of poverty dictating the lives of so many people.

As our programme reach deepened in the thirty-plus countries in which we operated, an additional element began to appear in our work. Once more, it arose from our close, day-to-day connection with our donor base, these mostly British, predominantly Muslim people focused on doing good rather than following any particular spiritual or political leadership. What they began to tell us was that they wanted to be of service at home as well as overseas. In part, I think, this was because the dramatic expansion in our overseas work had made people realise just how effective we were: if Penny Appeal could make such a difference in The Gambia, Gaza, Kashmir, what could they do here at home in the UK?

As we met our donors at events and spoke to them during fundraisers, we heard their concerns, time and again, about people in need at home in our own country – and not necessarily Muslims, either. This was colour- and faith-blind empathy at work, expressions of care towards all those in Britain who were not faring well, suffering from homelessness, poverty, mental illness, domestic abuse. *Why can't Penny Appeal also help these people?* we were asked.

We could. In January 2015, we launched our first UK programme under the banner of Love Thy Neighbour, which later became known as Penny Appeal at Home. The initial project was a soup kitchen where 840 meals were provided to the homeless in Manchester. I was pleased to welcome the help and support of world-champion boxer Amir Khan there. He stood behind the counters with our Team Orange volunteers and handed out food to the needy. At the end of that year, on 5 December, Storm Desmond broke; in twenty-four hours over thirteen inches of rain fell in Honister Pass in Cumbria, breaking the UK's twenty-four-hour rainfall record. The situation worsened very rapidly, and before long over 5,000 homes in Lancashire and Cumbria were flooded. We stepped in straight away, allocating funds from the Penny Appeal at Home programme to help families affected by the floods. An army of Team Orange volunteers flocked to Carlisle, Cumbria to help remove damaged items from flooded homes, host community lunches, provide activities for children. We delivered hundreds of food and cleaning packs to residents.

We stayed in touch with the people we helped and the organisations we worked with, and returned to Carlisle a number of times over the following months to provide further support. This included redecorating homes and community centres damaged by the floods, helping many of the victims who hadn't been able to afford high premiums, and thus weren't insured. Penny Appeal has since maintained links with the region, and to this day Team Orange volunteers work with local agencies in Cumbria to help the homeless as well as people unable to provide for their families. That's another defining aspect of our work: just as we stayed connected to the elders of Hathia Dhamial after starting our first project, so in the UK we don't just walk away from situations where we have become involved. The dreadful fire at Grenfell Tower in

As British as a Cup of Tea campaign, December 2017

"Our work in Britain has really helped to define our character, and to reinforce the fact that while we are a Muslim charity and proud of it, we are also a British organisation that values human life."

London in 2017 is another case in point: Penny Appeal teams were on the scene within hours of the fire starting, helping survivors and relatives, providing support and food, and still, in 2021, we have a presence in the local Grenfell community, offering any help that is needed.

Our work in Britain has really helped to define our character, and to reinforce the fact that while we are a Muslim charity and proud of it, we are also a British organisation that values human life at home as much as elsewhere in the world. We are committed to a non-sectarian outlook. During 2019, for example, we led twenty-three assemblies across eighteen primary schools around the UK, teaching children about the importance of respecting and celebrating people of different faiths, backgrounds and identities.

As our work here has grown, I am keen to see us spending almost as much on pressing needs here in Britain as we do in developing countries; I would love to see Penny Appeal committing to spend £1 in Britain for every £1 we spend overseas. Why? Because our donors live in communities here in Britain, where they see deprivation and inequality; they visit other parts of Britain, and can see how some people just don't have the resources or the abilities to cope. Our donors, after all, are the ones who have told us they want us to do something about it.

Four million children and adults in the UK are not properly fed by today's standards. Overall, one in five of Britons lives below the poverty line. The number of people going hungry in the UK is growing. Last year food banks fed nearly a million people. All that gives us additional motivation to continue raising more and more funds: the more work we do both overseas and in the UK, the more we become aware of just how much more there is to be done.

There are now many ways in which we support communities in Britain, through core programmes and direct response. Food provision is one core programme that is stepped up during Ramadan, given all its associations with food and fasting. During Ramadan 2019, we provided over 40,000 hot meals through soup kitchens and community *iftars* up and down Britain, and as the impact of the Covid-19 pandemic continues to affect people's livelihoods, it's likely that those numbers are going to increase. A second core programme is our professional domestic abuse support service: we have trained personnel at the end of the telephone line to provide counselling and support to people suffering from any form of abuse. Last year alone, the service received over 6,000 calls, and during the pandemic in 2020, we extended our telephone service to provide a listening line for anyone to call who was experiencing loneliness on account of isolation.

"Adam" (not his real name) had seen our telephone number on the Internet, and hadn't previously called a domestic abuse helpline before. He is a support worker, and told our specialist that he felt "silly" calling a service for advice and for someone to talk to, as during his working life *he* has always been the one that people seek out, to share their problems, get advice or just have a chat. But he felt he had no one to talk to about his own experiences. He came from a British Asian background, and feared that if anyone in his community were to find out about his difficulties coping, he would become a laughingstock; he felt he should be strong and silent. Adam took some time to open up about the reason for his call, but before long he spoke about how his wife was financially abusing him, and how he was letting this happen time and time again. She controlled his finances, and wanted his money to be spent on her and on the house. Adam spoke about how he had sold his car for a third of the price so he could buy some blinds that she insisted on having. He swore at himself when relaying this, but as the conversation unfolded, he became more and more comfortable discussing his emotions. His wife regularly threw him out of the house, and he told us he was scared he would end up on the street, homeless. He told us that when he bought his house, she had asked him to put it solely in her name – to which he agreed. He believed this lack of ownership was the reason she was using coercive control and being abusive towards him.

Adam didn't understand why he was being treated in this way. He admitted that he did everything at home so his wife didn't have to: he cooks, cleans and takes care of the children. He also has a son from a previous marriage, who has a learning disability and requires twenty-four-hour care. Our Team Orange specialist spoke to him about how early intervention can help prevent concerns and worries from becoming a crisis. He had been taught that a man does not show signs of weakness, or he will not be respected. Following a conversation with the Team Orange helpline, Adam said he no longer felt this way, and told us that he would continue to contact the helpline and discuss his feelings more regularly.

"It's amazing how much a trained, sympathetic ear can help people begin the process of reshaping their lives"

It's amazing how much a trained, sympathetic ear can help people begin the process of reshaping their lives.

Our carefully planned support work here at home in Britain also includes a programme to support Muslim women in prison. Whatever the reason you find yourself behind bars, our society wants you to emerge a better, stronger person, more able to contribute to the life of this country. But all too often, prison can be a lonely, frightening and alienating environment that doesn't foster the conditions for any kind of self-improvement.

"Aisha" (not her real name), forty-three, is an incarcerated single mother of three children. She had the added burden of learning that her mother had died during her prison sentence. Family members blamed Aisha's imprisonment for the deterioration of her mother's health, which sent her into a spiral of depression. Penny Appeal supported a local Khidmat Centre, which took on Aisha's case, paying for her to attend a one-day-a-week placement where she began to work on web-development projects. When her prison term was coming to an end, the Centre helped her find a house outside her hometown, and assisted with the supply of furniture through local charities.

Aisha said recently: "I have had a lot of trauma in my life, from domestic violence and abuse from my drug-addicted husband to my mum dying while I was in prison. It's hard to always be strong, and just when I was on the verge of giving

UK homeless distribution, Manchester 2020

up, the project helped me to pull myself together for the sake of my kids. Even the smallest of things I used to be able to do before looked like mountains upon my release. It is only through Penny Appeal's support that I have got the mental health support I needed, as well as the practical support. The project workers visit me two or even three times weekly, and they are on the other end of the phone. That really matters a lot, because I don't go out in public much – I can't stand the stares and the gossip I get."

Our direct response in support of vulnerable people in Britain is often visible in the form of the unmissable bright orange "Penny the Bus", a bright orange double-decker launched in 2016. Since then, it has been all over the UK, bringing Team Orange volunteers to visit schools, hospitals and senior care homes. In July 2016, the big orange bus was parked outside Great Ormond Street children's hospital in central London, delivering Eid gifts to young children. Later that year, Penny could be seen in different cities, providing a mobile haircutting service for homeless people.

The bus regularly drives to senior care homes up and down the country to bring tea, biscuits, entertainment – and Team Orange volunteers with friendly faces who are happy to sit with residents for a chat. The volunteers encourage residents to become involved in the organisation and delivery of the events, which gives them a strong sense of ownership and purpose. Working together, they bond with others in the care home, and have a monthly occasion to look forward to. At each event, our volunteers and staff spend time with the residents, socialising with them – something that is so important for alleviating loneliness.

Last year, we also launched The Big Orange Hug, in which Penny would be the focus of a range of services – haircutting, entertainment, medical reviews, hot meals and "pampering stations" – offered to vulnerable people including refugees and the homeless at events across London, Peterborough, Wakefield and Coventry.

On the coldest days of the year, Team Orange volunteers go out into cities and towns across the UK to distribute Winter Kits to homeless people. Handing out bags filled with warm clothing and hygiene essentials, they sit and talk with the homeless, empowering them to share their stories. Many of the recipients tell us how incredibly grateful they feel to receive these kind donations, with some admitting their fears that they might not otherwise have been able to survive the winter months. Our Winter Kits contain items such as a toothbrush, toothpaste, mouthwash, a waterproof jacket, deodorant, a thermal top, thermal bottoms, socks, a hat, a scarf, body wash, wipes. Their distribution is now an essential part of our work and our reputation; our donors have seen that we are supporting and caring for those in need in our own country. This aspect of Penny Appeal's work will only increase as the organisation continues to grow.

○

Our sense of belonging, of being British and Muslim, has been with us from the start. We regularly used the phrase *Confidently Muslim, Comfortably British* in our communications, and ran a successful press campaign based on it that attracted more donor support. Then, in 2017, after the earlier success with Omar Regan and *American Sharia*, we had an opportunity to venture into a specifically British film project. I was keen for the charity to support a new film that would mirror the success we had with Omar in raising funds, but which also did more to reflect our Britishness. Omar's film was tremendous, but it was set in Los Angeles. Could we reflect the lives of our donors, our supporters and our families with a creative project that would also inspire donations? We found the answer in a new collaboration with the team at British Muslim TV, which decided to fund the production of a new British romantic comedy called *Finding Fatimah*.

The script was written by Manchester-based teacher-turned-filmmaker Oz Arshad, and told the story of Shahid, a divorced British Muslim man juggling all kinds of contemporary issues: stigma about his failed marriage, a day job selling computer printers, his aspirations to make it as a stand-up comedian on TV shows such as the invented *Muslims with Talent* and, above all, his wish to find the love of his life. The tangles of his blossoming relationship with hard-working GP Fatimah formed an accurate picture of day-to-day life for many British Muslims. As with *American Sharia*, Penny Appeal secured the touring rights for the movie, and we planned a nineteen-city tour using our familiar format of family-friendly ticket prices, a professional fundraising element and the screening of the movie itself.

I was thrilled to attend the premiere in London. The cinema was packed; the queue to get in stretched all the way across Leicester Square. It was such a Penny Appeal sight, with cheerful Muslim families and young women on an evening out mingling with non-Muslim British viewers. As usual, our Team Orange volunteers were out in force, handing out leaflets about the focus of our fundraising that night, the emergency crisis taking place in East Africa that year. Once we were all in our seats, comedian Kae Kurd kicked the evening off with a crowd-pleasing show that emphasised the need for positive messaging in the British Muslim community. Then the redoubtable Rahim Jung took to the stage to tell the audience about Penny Appeal's work in East Africa, and set the bar high by asking if anyone wished to begin the bidding at £20,000.

Within half an hour, with audience pledges ranging from £50 to £10,000, Rahim raised £100,000 for the charity. Incredible! It was exactly the same format we had perfected two years earlier, only this time our audience, now settling in their seats with the knowledge that they had supported people in need, was able to watch a completely British romantic comedy with a British Muslim production team and stars. It was one of those nights I shall always remember. More importantly, the financial return to date on that film has been over £600,000.

I took Mum to see *Finding Fatimah* when the tour came to Wakefield. The storyline reminded us both of long, long ago, when she would prop up grainy black-and-white photographs of one or another of my cousins in Pakistan on the mantelpiece. We chuckled about the memory, but as usual, she had some advice for me:

"Don't forget, Adeem," she said. "You *come from this city*. You are doing good things, I'm proud of you. Just make sure you keep it up. There is always someone, some poor soul in our own city, who needs our help."

I never tire of emphasising that it is our Britishness as much as our Muslim-ness that defines Penny Appeal. We adhere to the tenets of our faith, and have specific programmes such as our Mosque Project (for donations towards mosque-building where needed), which are clearly very specifically aimed at the Muslim community around the world. But at the same time, we are proud to be British, and take delight in participating in traditions such as a Leicester Square premiere. Penny Appeal grew out of my hometown, and it's never going to move away from Wakefield. It's where I grew up, where I live now, where my family is … Mum still lives in the same house I grew up in. I can no more imagine Penny Appeal relocating from Wakefield than I can imagine myself leaving, either. Without roots, how does a tree grow?

CHAPTER ELEVEN

PAINTING THE WORLD ORANGE

The "skinny little Paki" who was always getting into scrapes in that street of terraced houses, diving into skips to recycle unwanted tennis racquets, making fires on the waste ground and watching white friends sip cider from cans – well, he never really thought much about the great big world outside of Wakefield. Little Adeem saw the world much as his mum and grandad did: it was bordered by those few streets, where uncles and aunties lived next door and women gathered together in the kitchen preparing supper while men returned home each evening from working in the factory. We knew of the wider world from stories at the mosque about the life of the Holy Prophet, Peace Be Upon Him, and from occasional glimpses on TV of glamorous Bollywood stars. All my male Pakistani friends in Wakefield had the inbuilt assumption that they would follow in their fathers' footsteps and drive taxis, or work in a restaurant or a factory. And while I didn't have that example of my own to look up to, I still didn't have much of an idea about what the rest of the world was like. I think it's the same if you grow up poor anywhere: your mental horizons are limited to your day-to-day surroundings, because each day throws up challenges that occupy most of your attention when you don't have quite enough money to get by. *Travel the world?* I couldn't even afford bus fare.

My first glimpse of the outside world, at twelve, was when Grandad first took me to Pakistan. But it still didn't occur to me that I might one day travel to other continents. I lasted only a month at university in Newcastle before coming back home, quite unable to accommodate my thinking to living away from Wakefield. Even now, when I'm landing at Heathrow or Manchester Airport, I have that genuine sense of excitement that I'll be back in Wakefield before too long. I've got many good friends in London, and wonderful Penny Appeal donors there; but if I'm honest, the view I like best of our capital is when it's in the rear-view mirror of my car as I head home. Like many people of Pakistani descent, we didn't really do the whole 'holiday' thing; even now, I usually have to be forced to book a vacation in the sun; it's just not a big priority for me. Call it learned behaviour, but it runs deep.

Thus my discovery of the world has taken a more practical form, akin to the way in which I first learned about the worlds of work and business as a kid at the ITV studios in Leeds. I've never done any romantic "hopping on a train and wandering around Europe"; I've just gone to places where I needed to get something done, like flying out to Los Angeles to check on Omar Regan: I needed to be sure our film was on track, and it didn't really occur to me that I was visiting the home of the American movie industry. I did like the palm trees, though.

○

By 2015, when Penny Appeal was becoming a serious force and raising almost £10 million that year, we began to see that rapid growth was going to bring more and more responsibilities with it. We were now responsible for the lives of orphans, vulnerable older people, people in need of fresh water or proper eye health care. We were going to have to look after those orphans for years; we couldn't allow anything untoward to happen, which might threaten our ability to continue supporting them. But what if something *did* happen? What if, for some reason upon which I couldn't speculate on at that point, Penny Appeal couldn't continue raising funds? What would those children do then?

There seemed, to me, to be a practical solution: begin to build replicas of Penny Appeal around the world, so that in the event of any failure to raise enough money here in the UK, we could still fund our global programmes by raising it elsewhere – a kind of insurance policy against a UK "donation crash". It was

"Even now, when I'm landing at Heathrow or Manchester Airport, I have that genuine sense of excitement that I'll be back in Wakefield before too long."

a hard-headed business decision, not dissimilar to my thinking behind the expansion of Single Muslim to other countries. No entrepreneur ever ignores a potential market for what they offer, after all. We had discovered how enthusiastically British Muslim donors responded to, and were grateful for, the affordable and rewarding charitable programmes we offered them; how many more potential donors might there be elsewhere in the world?

It was an exciting revelation. Urban Muslims around the world might appreciate the ethos and DNA of Penny Appeal: small-change-big-difference, Muslim and Western, in tune with global trends. Globalisation had made the world a smaller place; younger generations of Muslims now had very similar cultural reference points, whether they were in Sydney, San Francisco or Swindon. They approached their faith on similar lines, followed the same inspirational spiritual teachers on social media, watched the same films, bought the same brands. The emergence of this new identity meant that the Penny Appeal formula that was tried and tested here was likely to take off in other parts of the world, too.

So, in 2016, off we went to the US. That's where all ambitious Brits head first, from the Beatles onwards: it's the land of opportunity, right? I toured several key American states with our CEO, the Sheikh, visited some major Muslim expos, learned how Muslims tick Stateside, what the benefits offered to donors were, how the charity sector operates over there and who future potential competitors would be. It's very different, obviously; there's no equivalent of the UK regulator, the Charity Commission, and charitable organisations there are treated just like any commercial organisation, except they are given tax-exemption status.

Penny Appeal USA was registered as a tax-exempt, non-profit organisation early in 2016. We found and appointed a chief executive, and established a sort of licensing agreement allowing PA USA to use the Penny Appeal brand and logo, graphics and all campaign materials. The UK operation incubated its sister organisation in the US with initial cashflow, so it could hit the ground running. In return, PA USA agreed to allocate 50 per cent of funds raised in the US to support existing Penny Appeal UK projects around the world, as well as an equivalent to our "at home" programme. We had been very clear in our self-description of Penny Appeal in the UK – that we were "confidently Muslim, comfortably British". I now wanted Penny Appeal offices abroad to feel they could adopt the same slogan: "confidently Muslim, comfortably Canadian", or "... comfortably Australian". This was an important cultural narrative that we fed through our developing global network, an important concept that would enable the new Penny Appeal branches to distinguish themselves from previous-generation Islamic charities in the same energetic way we had done in the UK. By 2020, Penny Appeal USA was sending our global programmes more money than we had spent setting it up.

In July 2021, Penny Appeal USA will celebrate its fifth anniversary with a special campaign highlighting all we've achieved over the last five years. All the basics that we set up when Penny Appeal was no more than an idea and a desk in my

"The international network is a significant next stage of the Penny Appeal story."

office back in 2009, from colours and tagline to programmes, can all be found on the PA USA website. It's so exciting to see how our charity has taken root in the US, and even more exciting to forecast how PA USA and our other satellite offices are going to continue to expand using the methodologies and philosophies we pioneered in the UK. Every time I visited one of our orphan homes in Pakistan or Sudan, the fear that something might happen to our UK revenue, that we would not be able to continue to fund them, would strike me. Now Penny Appeal USA has proved that the licensing model can work. The grants and training we committed for it to roll out the orange DNA in the USA were worth the investment and hard work. I now feel reassured that we have provided additional security for those children. The international network is a significant next stage of the Penny Appeal story.

The operating environment for Penny Appeal in the US is, of course, very different to that in the UK. For a start, the Muslim presence in the US is composed of different origins. My mum and dad were typical Pakistani arrivals in Britain, but the US never saw the arrival of a whole generation of Muslims from former colonies to work in relatively low-paid jobs in factories or restaurants. The Muslim community in the US is made up more of recent arrivals, and often professionals emigrating from countries all over the world, attracted to the US by the economic opportunity, receiving Green Cards indicating their value as economic contributors. They are engineers, scientists, academics, businesspeople. The Muslim donor community in the US is, as a percentage of the population, smaller compared to the UK; but it is probably also significantly wealthier. The community there is spread more widely all over that massive country, and there isn't that sense of tightly-knit British Muslim communities such as those in Wakefield, Birmingham, East London and so on. The TV culture is very different in the US, too, of course; it would have been difficult to replicate the success there that we had in the UK with the British Muslim TV fundraising specials.

Thus Penny Appeal USA operates differently, focusing more on big national trade events in Chicago, Los Angeles and New York; working within the US employment system, by which employers can match your voluntary donations; setting up innovative US-style fundraisers featuring activities such as bubble soccer. There's no doubt, though, about the effectiveness: the most recently published report for PA USA showed revenue of over US$6 million dollars for 2019 – remarkable, given that the office only launched formally three years earlier. As with Penny Appeal in the UK, it appears that revenue is only going in one direction – up – with amazing average annual growth of 60 per cent. In just four years, the donor database for Penny Appeal USA grew from zero to 60,000 individuals.

Penny Appeal USA has followed many of the UK fundraising innovations, such as music and comedy tours, even with UK features. In 2020, we raised funds in aid of Penny Appeal's work in Palestine by touring award-winning British Muslim film director Abrar Hussain's second movie *One Night in Al-Aqsa* across ten US cities. This was another film funded by Penny

Appeal UK to help make it possible. With the donations raised, Al Makassed Hospital in Jerusalem will be able to expand its imaging-radiology department and neonatal unit through the renovation of the existing site, allowing the hospital to serve 450–600 inpatients a year.

The tradition of Penny Appeal volunteers exists in the US too, with Team Orange set up in major cities all over the country, going out into the community to help the vulnerable and setting up evening game nights to raise funds.

Penny Appeal USA has broadened the international reach of the charity. And just as we aim to keep increasing our donor spend on projects at home in Britain, so our American colleagues have been able to identify needs closer to them: for example, with over 20,000 refugees settling in the US in 2018, PA USA has established a programme to help refugee families and communities restart their lives after a period of displacement. When Hurricane Maria caused such chaos in Puerto Rico in 2017, PA USA provided shelter-restoration kits for the worst-hit homes in the Barranquitas region. In 2020, PA USA distributed over US$1.5 million to American families affected by the Covid-19 pandemic as well. Last year, over 25 per cent of the PA USA spend was on vulnerable American beneficiaries, helping Americans at home just as we help fellow Britons here at home.

Also, in 2016, we set up Penny Appeal Australia as an independent charity in that country, with the same user agreement in place with Penny Appeal UK as with the US. In its first year of operations, it recorded income of AUD$700,000, rising to over AUD$4 million in its fourth year. It has been hugely satisfying to see these levels of growth – particularly so in Australia, where the small team in Sydney has been so effective at using social media to connect with young people all over the country; much of this impressive level of revenue

Penny Appeal Team USA, July 2019

comes from millennials. Australia is a vast country, but 250 Team Orange volunteers now operate from one end of it to the other, supplying food banks and soup kitchens and setting up domestic abuse helplines.

As we have seen in other countries, Penny Appeal Australia has already made a visible impact on the lives of vulnerable people. During the Covid-19 crisis, it gave out over 5,000 hot meals to the homeless and the elderly. And when the country suffered so badly from raging bush fires in 2020, Penny Appeal Australia engaged with six rural fire services to make sure they were supplied with energy drinks, water and food. Penny Appeal Australia also works internationally on projects that our UK team has not initiated, and on innovative projects, such as the funding of a bakery in Yemen: we are trying to establish more permanent solutions in crisis-hit areas, and longer-term, sustainable ways for vulnerable people to maintain a living. It looks like the success of the charity in Australia in its first four years will deliver even more growth in revenue over the coming years. Already, just like Penny Appeal USA, our sister operation in Australia has sent more money out for international programme work than it has received in incubation funds from us.

Penny Appeal had a presence in Pakistan from the start, with Habib Nawaz providing such thoughtful and intelligent leadership. The office there operates as a branch of the UK charity, rather than taking the American or Australian licence model, and we decided to follow this route in 2018 when we established another branch office, this time in Dubai. It took quite a long time to complete all the Dubai regulatory requirements, so we weren't fully operational until at least the middle of 2019. Yet even so, following the dynamic pattern of our global offices, Dubai Penny Appeal raised almost US$1 million dollars during its first full trading year, 2020.

Eighty per cent of Dubai's population consists of expatriates – very different from the UK, US and Australia. It's a much more transient society; residents stay there for three or four years before leaving to work in another country. There are plenty of strategic reasons for Penny Appeal to have opened an office in this Middle Eastern country: it is a key staging post for travellers to and from the Indian subcontinent and Africa, and there are about five million Indian and Pakistani expats living in the country at any one time. Penny Appeal will have a presence alongside other charities and NGOs at Expo 2020, the World Expo being hosted by Dubai in 2021–22 (the postponement was on account of the coronavirus pandemic). It will be a major international platform for us to highlight our work across the world. The emirate is a convenient meeting point for people from all over the world; we held our first Penny Appeal global CEO conference in Dubai.

Fundraising regulations in Dubai require permits to be

Penny Appeal South Africa, July 2017

obtained for each campaign, so together with the very specific nature of the population, our fundraising there is less aimed at the general public and more at high-net-worth individuals and corporations. This means that often, funds are provided for specific projects rather than for more general campaigns: a wealthy individual may contact us with a proposal to fund a school in Bangladesh, for instance. Also, Dubai rules stipulate that foreign agencies – such as Penny Appeal's office there – cannot engage in local works. As our Dubai revenue grows, we shall likely partner with local agencies in the emirate to allocate grants supporting vulnerable groups there.

As elsewhere, the Dubai office has used the Penny Appeal tradition of live events as a means of spreading awareness of the charity. Early in 2020, multi-award-winning British comedian and actor Paul Chowdhry performed a series of shows, his first in the United Arab Emirates, across multiple venues in the UAE on a tour organised by the Dubai office, called "Comedy-4-A-Cause". Chowdhry performed at Vox Cinemas Cineplex Grand Hyatt and at the American University of Sharjah, joined by UAE-based Mina Liccione, co-founder of Dubomedy; Emirati comedian Ali Al Sayed; and MB14, beatboxer and *The Voice* finalist. Comedy-4-A-Cause raised funds for Penny Appeal's Back to School project in South Africa, which provides students from impoverished communities with essential learning resources.

Six thousand kilometres away in Durban, South Africa, a hybrid model of a Penny Appeal international office was opened in 2018. The scenario in southern Africa is also different from all other PA branches. In the countries of southern Africa, there is a polarity of life experience: wealth pertains to a small minority of people, with the vast majority living difficult lives beset by poverty. Southern Africa has what may be the highest numbers of orphan children in the world, so from a humanitarian perspective – from the perspective of Penny Appeal's fundamental vision – there was a clear need for us to be able to operate in this region. For these reasons, Penny Appeal South Africa probably has more operational and field responsibilities than PA in other countries.

The office in Durban has been successful in its first two years, attracting institutional and grant funding to support its humanitarian work. It needs to be able to do this, because the potential for fundraising in a country with so much indigenous poverty is more challenging than in some other countries. South Africa is arguably the hub country of what is known as the Southern African Development Community (SADC), which is made up of Angola, Botswana, Comoros, Congo-Kinshasa, Eswatini, Lesotho, Madagascar, Malawi, Mozambique, Namibia, Seychelles, South Africa, Tanzania, Zambia and Zimbabwe. The SADC is committed to alleviating poverty, and there are thousands of NGOs in South Africa at work in the wider region. Thus we see Penny Appeal South Africa as an important signifier of our commitment to expand our own humanitarian work in the coming years into countries where we have not yet operated.

Muslims constitute no more than 5 per cent of the population of South Africa, so in terms of fundraising there is quite a steep hill for our team to climb. Even so, with the addition of the grant support received, Penny Appeal South Africa is growing. At the same time, that 5 per cent tends to be several generations long in terms of residency in South Africa: they are South African, born and bred. We shall aim to win their confidence by demonstrating the effectiveness of our charitable work in SADC countries. It is effective, for example, when potential donors there see the impact of local Penny Appeal activities such as the Breakfast Club, which provides nutritious breakfasts to poor children who otherwise would be going to school with empty stomachs.

Finally, 2019 saw the opening of Penny Appeal Canada, which has followed the model of PA in other countries by leaping into action straight away. In its first year, it raised an astonishing CAD$4 million, and is set to continue that growth moving forwards. As elsewhere, Penny Appeal Canada focuses on issues close to home, working with communities, for example, to provide school equipment for low-income families. (In an empathetic touch, the Team Orange volunteers asked recipients to choose what items their children needed, rather than giving out products top-down.) Penny Appeal Canada has also been tremendous at engaging high-profile national and international celebrities and public figures to support its work, and was even featured in a public event with Canadian Prime Minister Justin Trudeau. For such a young charity to be making such a significant impact really fills me with hope for the future.

In just a few years, the Penny Appeal global family has achieved more than I might have expected when we first visualised it in 2016. It has opened up our core charitable programmes around the world to further funding support – a crucial addition to our UK funding base. Now, we can be assured that we won't have to depend 100 per cent on British donors for our global work, which is a useful backstop; at the same time, it's my intention to grow our income in the UK considerably, and as we do that, we shall surely see similar growth occurring in our offices around the world. We may only have been in existence for just over ten years, but we are now a global operation in every way.

Our international orange family will also engage with us more into the future, identifying areas of poverty and need beyond our traditional countries of operation – so as we boost our overall charitable income, we shall have more urgent projects and programmes in which to invest our donors' money. Team Orange will be seen in more places, more often, for as long as we are needed. Just as we have done in the UK for our first ten years, we are going to spend the next ten years painting the world orange, motivating our volunteers all over the world, engaging with our donors in more and more countries as we grow the international network. It's such an exciting prospect.

CHAPTER TWELVE

GROWING UP

As I write this, in December 2020, we're just signing off the Penny Appeal accounts for the year ending 30 April 2020. For my fellow trustees, whose responsibility it is to oversee the actions of the charity, that is an onerous responsibility. We are putting our names to the actions and statements of the organisation, confirming to the Charity Commission that our house is in good order. I am happy to say, after a period of some turbulence (which I shall tell you about soon), that our house is in better order than it has ever been. As I reflect on that, I am able to see once more just how far we have come, and how we have grown in so many ways.

When we first started out, I hadn't got much further than knowing I needed to create a formal and legal structure to honour the wishes of people such as David Taylor, who had offered his support to the work I was funding in Pakistan. I had already come to the conclusion that a charitable structure would enable me to do much more than I could achieve as an individual, but it was David's remarkable gesture that pushed me into taking the first steps.

I then asked a freelance copywriter I employed from time to time, Jo Marshall, to brief me on what I needed to do to set up a charity. Jo is a highly intelligent, diligent professional. Not only did she explain clearly to me the processes we needed to undertake, she also did me the honour of agreeing to be one of the first trustees of Penny Appeal. She was joined by my wife, Dr Shama Firdous, who, despite combining the demands of a busy GP surgery with the arrival of our firstborn, generously offered her time and wise counsel to the young charity.

The can-do attitude of both women, representing two thirds of our inaugural board, was typical of Penny Appeal. In fact, Jo's husband Chris joined in, too: in 2009, he raised nearly £700 for us by taking part in the Admiral Swansea 10,000-Kilometre Run, despite only having taken up running in April of that year. His funds helped 200 people in need in the Konsh Valley. Chris smashed his own record two years later by creating the Run2012 challenge, in which he agreed to run an eye-watering 2,012 kilometres in 2012 to raise money for Penny Appeal – working out an average of one marathon every week of the year! His target was to raise £12,000, and he did, helping to fund twelve clean water wells in Afghanistan, Bangladesh, The Gambia, India, Indonesia, Kashmir, Nepal, Niger, Pakistan, Somalia, Sri Lanka and Sudan. Jo, making a tireless contribution as a trustee from 2009–15, and Chris, in his own determined way, symbolised the true spirit of this great charity as well as the genuine diversity we've had from the top since our inception.

Next, to recap, came sign-off from the Charity Commission, an increase of activity in Pakistan, the arrival of Rizwan Khaliq, longer-term programmes, exponential growth, a greater presence online and via live television and events. The Penny Appeal brand became more deeply embedded in the public consciousness; that's how brands develop, as I had learned from my own commercial experience, and it was satisfying to see Penny Appeal gaining traction as the rules of successful brand management began to take hold. It wasn't just a matter of a bright orange logo: brands with staying power offer real meaning to people, an emotional truth. They encapsulate elements about our lives that resonate widely. Apple isn't a brand because it has a cool logo and some very slickly designed pieces of kit: it represents a whole psychological and emotional outlook for its consumers, who keep going back to it. Brands are for life, not just for Ramadan.

Penny Appeal's "marketing-led" brand has been anchored by our wish to listen clearly and actively to what our donors tell us they want us to achieve on their behalf. We exist to connect donors and recipients; we are a vehicle for implementation. For

"Penny Appeal's "marketing-led" brand has been anchored by our wish to listen clearly and actively to what our donors tell us they want us to achieve on their behalf."

us, marketing means precisely this two-way communication, which ensures complete transparency as to how donor funds are being used.

From the start, we prided ourselves on giving more emphasis to donor communication than many other charities. When we began to train telephone operators in the "nursery", we emphasised that donors must be allowed to talk through the issues that were of importance to them – honouring a deceased relative, needing to understand how to complete *zakat* effectively, whether or not we could allocate more money to, say, Palestine or Pakistan.

Our message was that you might not be a wealthy person, but we promise to use whatever you can give us to make visible improvements in people's lives. You've lost a grandparent? Perhaps the Adopt-a-Gran programme might be of interest. Your cousin in Pakistan has no running water? Let's look at our Thirst Relief programme. It was never about just asking for money and then dispensing it as we saw fit. We now have an efficient and dedicated donor liaison team that guarantees donors information on what has been done with their money. We never accept payments and then turn our backs, and we have a range of mechanisms in place now to ensure that can't happen.

As we have matured as an organisation, and as the world has continued to change, we have also absorbed lessons that many other charities are now beginning to take on board. One lesson we have learned through experience is to observe "localisation", a rather fancy word meaning that the views, thoughts and aspirations of recipients in developing countries *must take precedence*. When that twelve-year-old girl in Sohawa, Rafia Bi, first told us that she wanted to leave the orphan home we had created for her and her sisters and go back to the filthy barn where they had been living, she taught me a lesson I have never forgotten: we cannot impose top-down solutions on the developing world; we must listen and respond to what the recipients of aid tell us they need, what's important to them. Surprisingly – from the Western perspective – it's not always financial assistance.

Therefore, it's unsurprising that Penny Appeal today fully embraces global humanitarian calls for reform such as the Charter for Change, which encourages more locally-led responses to developing-country needs. We have always worked closely with local delivery partners, and where possible we have employed people on the ground to act as our eyes and ears. As Habib first taught me in Pakistan, it is vital for a UK-based charity to be responsive to local need rather than offer distant solutions. Now one of the core functions of our donor support team is to have people from the programme teams discuss the latest thinking from the relevant countries about what is needed.

One very moving example of this process was when a young man called Ruhith Wadi contacted the team. Ruhith told us that he and his family had lost his father to Covid-19 on 2 April 2020. Unable to be with his father during his last hours because of his own requirement to self-isolate with his mother, who was poorly, Ruhith was understandably devastated. Showing remarkable strength of character, he chose to honour his much-loved father by doing something to commemorate the latter's joy spending time in his local mosque in Ilford, London. Ruhith decided to donate *sadaqah* (non-obligatory charity) himself in order to finance the building of a mosque in his father's memory.

He came to our Head of Fundraising, Ridwana Wallace Laher, and explained his wish. Ridwana, one of our most experienced, sympathetic and professional senior team members, immediately discussed the matter with the Programmes team. In the previous twelve months, we had provided funds for the construction of thirty-two mosques around the world as part of our Mosque Project programme. The team informed Ridwana that a rural district called Yumbe, over 500 kilometres north of Kampala, Uganda, needed a mosque, which in turn needed to be part of a sustainable water and food production area: the local people, suffering from the effects of climate change, had become reliant on aid for food. They wanted to break their dependence on aid, but didn't have the wherewithal.

Here was a wonderful and inspiring example of how our donors work alongside the recipients in developing countries to deliver a project that meets their specific and expressed needs. Ruhith decided to expand his own generosity by raising more funds himself through a JustGiving campaign in partnership with Penny Appeal. As a result, he managed to garner a remarkable £35,778 to build the mosque, which would be fully outfitted according to the specifications of the local people. It was to have exterior paved areas for outdoor prayers and activities; solar panels on the roof for electricity; a distinct and separate female prayer section; an outdoor *wudhu* (ablutions) area; a deep water well installed for clean water; and a sustainable community vegetable garden. Moreover, it would offer skilled training in diversified agricultural farming methods, to allow local people to pursue their food-security ambitions.

Here was a humbling example of the way our donors are able to reach out over thousands of miles to link up with recipients meaningfully.

Another example, closer to home: Humayun Islam runs the BEAP Community Partnership in Bradford, which provides support for people suffering from high levels of deprivation in and around the Manningham area of the city. They have a centre not far from the Bradford City football ground, where residents can walk in and seek help and advice. During the coronavirus pandemic in 2020, they had to close down some of their walk-in services, which left them with the problem of how to get help to people in need. They began to deliver food packs to vulnerable older people in the community, working in partnership with local temples and other community groups as well as private supporters. Humayun already knew us, as he had given generously to Penny Appeal several times in the past; he was delighted when Ridwana reached out and told him that Penny Appeal had received donor support for the provision of UK help, and would it be useful if we were to supply the food packs for BEAP to distribute? By the end of March 2020, very soon into the first lockdown, Penny Appeal began supplying food packs to BEAP weekly.

Humayun says: "This made a massive difference. It meant that we could get food to our elderly clients, many of whom lived alone in sheltered accommodation and who simply couldn't risk going out. It's been a real lifeline. And although Penny Appeal probably could have used their own Team Orange volunteers to give the food out, it was really helpful that they collaborated with us, because our clients knew and trusted us and preferred to receive support from people they already knew. We've been operating in Bradford for twenty years, so it was really great that Penny Appeal supported us and allowed us to take the lead in food distribution."

Although much of our work is with older, vulnerable people around the world and in the UK, we have also had a big emphasis on youth – particularly with the OrphanKind programme (which is, of course, close to my heart). We have been youthful, too, in our public profile, in our embrace of contemporary British culture and by installing ourselves in cities; we have never wanted to be an aloof organisation, unable to connect with ordinary people.

I shall always resist attempts to prise us from our roots amongst the young and the old alike in our communities. But at the same time, over these ten years, Penny Appeal has matured in important ways, learning from our recipients in countries around the world and from our programme partners (who are all listed in the Appendix to this book). We have evolved from a charity that simply brought aid to where it was needed to one that now works on sustainable programmes around the world. We deliver food parcels as part of Feed Our World, but we also now provide communities with instruction on climate-resilient farming techniques, and seeds for growing crops in abundance. We train women in agriculture, empower communities to grow their own food and sell crops, providing a livelihood as well as access to year-round, nutrient-dense food.

In The Gambia, we have purchased 400 plots of land in the region of Tamba Kunda, and have been training women from the villages where the plots are located, providing them with the tools they need to reap the maximum results. We conduct training on a variety of topics, enabling them to adapt their farming style to suit the changing climate. An agricultural technician supports the project, providing expert advice whenever needed. The women plant and harvest a range of crops year-round and sell their produce to a local vendor, who takes them to market. They also keep enough nutritious fruit and vegetables to feed their families and give to their neighbours. The women learn how to preserve their crops, ensuring they have enough food to see them through periods of harsh weather. They are now able to save money for their children, grow crops despite the changeable weather and feed their families enough to support healthy growth and development.

Another example recently stopped me in my tracks, and I couldn't help but think of my own mother. Saadia Shamali lives in al-Shajaiya, east of Gaza City in Palestine. She is the mother of five sons. After her husband's death, she became the sole breadwinner of the family. She rented agricultural land and planted it with seasonal crops such as chickpeas and okra. She found it difficult to irrigate the crops because of a lack of a suitable irrigation network, and her income remained low. However, she applied for assistance from a Penny Appeal-supported organisation called Taawon, which supports solutions that enable women to live with dignity. Now she has access to a reliable irrigation network and a wider range of seeds, and provides for her family through a sustainable agricultural living, which was her ambition to begin with. My admiration for people like Saadia knows no bounds; that we were able to support her initiative, courage and positivity gives me immense satisfaction.

Ten years on, we are able to combine short-term aid during emergencies and climate crises such as harvest failures with long-term, sustainable food interventions, which help to free communities around the world from their dependence on foreign aid. The same joined-up thinking informs our other programmes: while we're building over 8,000 new fresh water wells every year through our Thirst Relief programme, we're also building solar-energy water and power centres for villages

Solar Panel and Power Centre,
Tharparkar, Pakistan 2020

to access water at any time, day or night. We recognise the need for education on sanitation to ensure that water is collected and stored safely, and for communities to improve hygiene. We run awareness sessions on topics such as handwashing and water storage, helping communities stay healthy and protected from preventable illnesses and waterborne diseases.

Similarly, our orphan care has developed extensively since those five little girls came to live at the home in Sohawa. Now, though we sponsor thousands of new orphan homes around the world annually, we have also developed close working relationships with partner agencies in different countries to allow us to intervene at a more structural level. For example, in Bangladesh we've set up over 100 literacy centres across the Sylhet slums, allowing children to have access to free education provided by experienced teachers in classrooms that have proper facilities for learning. (We have conducted teacher training to ensure that all staff are fully qualified.) We also supply the children with school uniforms and shoes, and have carried out distributions of hygiene kits, too. They enjoy the hygiene awareness sessions, and proudly share what they learn with their families, so we are thus able to reach many more people in the community. The centres are busy, creative environments that have inspired thousands of children.

We now routinely go out into problem areas to address the difficulties facing street children, who are forced to beg and are regularly subject to terrible abuse. We have our own outreach workers in Bangladesh, Pakistan, Lebanon and Senegal, experts on child trauma who work sensitively to understand the diverse needs of children living in the streets; they work on the children's terms, building trust and supporting them at their own pace. We also have rescue centres that have been designed to get children out of danger as quickly as possible. Our staff then work with them and their families, reuniting

Education First programme, Uganda 2020

them where possible and continuing to support them with food, medicine and education to ensure that they stay off the streets. In Senegal, we've been running a radio campaign to educate the community on children's rights. We have invited students to take part in the recordings, giving them a voice and a platform from which to advocate for themselves. It has been a very empowering process. We have also provided the children with vocational training sessions to supplement their education and prepare them for employment. Most of this work happens through our network of vetted expert partners, who have been on the ground for many years and work with local actors. We leverage their collective experiences and connections, empowering the right people and supplementing local economies.

Growing up, Mum told me more than once, is about accepting responsibility. Penny Appeal does accept the responsibility that comes from intervening in other people's lives. Many international charities have been criticised for imposing solutions from above in developing countries, even those with global profiles such as Comic Relief – which, over the last couple of years, has been accused of using wealthy white people to figurehead the undoubtedly good work it conducts on the ground. Worse, there have been too many stories of personnel directly employed by major charities behaving in unacceptable ways towards those they are supposed to be looking after. Penny Appeal, inevitably, will get some things wrong, given the massive workload we now undertake; but we take a mature and responsible attitude towards the care we give.

One key application of that principle is the idea of *empowerment*. It is no longer enough for us to supply financial solutions where there is need; now, wherever we work, our objective is to empower communities to lift themselves out of poverty. In addition to building schools so that children can gather somewhere for their education rather than risk their health in severe climates by learning outdoors, we also work with adults in terms of vocational training, raising awareness on topics such as health, hygiene, gender-based violence and infant nutrition.

We have been involved in a major empowerment project in Nepal, working at a deeply sustainable level with an extremely marginalised community in the mainly Muslim district of Rautahat, where women are very vulnerable. We worked with the community all the way up to government level, advocating for Rautahat's women and providing them with access to livelihoods. We began by addressing the fact that foreign-born women there are often refused citizenship on account of societal fear that they will gain increased rights and access to land. We worked closely with the local government and male community leaders, who eventually granted citizenship to forty women. We then set up several training programmes for beauticians, seamstresses and electric-rickshaw drivers, in which many women enrolled – often with the full support of their families, who had received awareness training on women's rights and the importance of access to livelihoods. The women gained the respect of their community, becoming empowered members of their households. The beautician graduates began to spread awareness on the importance of good hygiene, and were looked up to as sources of inspiration.

In the Vehari district of Punjab, Pakistan, we have recently been engaged in much more long-term thinking about how to help the 30 per cent of the 2.8 million people there who live below the poverty line. Their problems are many, but of paramount influence is the climate. The district is agriculture-dependent; the majority of the population earn their livelihood through agriculture. However, it is subject to extremes of weather, including high temperatures and heavy rainfall. Smallholder farmers tend to have limited resources and capacity to cope with shocks, and any setbacks in their production can lead to food insecurity, lack of nutrition and reduced income. We identified an urgent need for these communities to learn adaptable methods of farming in order to boost their resilience and reduce their vulnerability to climate change.

To this end, we leased six acres of land in the district and selected women from three villages to take part in our Woman Open Schools: six schools in three villages, with over 100 women participating. The primary aim was to train women in small-scale farming techniques, and to teach them how to get the most out of their crops. Participants learned the various developmental stages of their crops through the yearlong initiative, gaining hands-on experience. They were trained right from the beginning of the process, in topics such as land preparation, seed germination and appropriate responses to signs of disease and pests. By learning through doing, the women could share their knowledge and experience with others. As the farmland is in the centre of the villages, other farmers indirectly benefited by observing the new techniques and learning from the women's experience.

In 2020, for the very first time, we took our Women's Welfare programme to South America, where we worked with ten women's entrepreneurial groups in Paraíba, Brazil. We empowered 250 women from Paraíba to get the most out of their businesses, providing them with training in business management, marketing and quality control, as well as supplying them with equipment and various materials. This project helped them cultivate more sustainable livelihoods, taking and maintaining control of their own economic development.

"Now, as I enter the fifth decade of my life and count my many, many blessings, maybe I can finally say that I have grown up along with Penny Appeal."

Just a few years ago, when I was already in my late thirties, my uncle Jehangir from Wembley said in front of his family: "Look at Adeem. He's built a business that has made him and his family financially secure. He's built a charity that helps millions of people all over the world."

I was embarrassed, of course, but Uncle was in full flow, and wouldn't be stopped.

"And you know why he's been so successful? Because he didn't have a dad. You children, you have me to sort everything out for you; you rely on me for your daily bread. You'll be relying on me forever if you don't buck your ideas up. Take a leaf out of your cousin Adeem's book."

I was cross with my uncle that evening. I didn't like the fact he had brought all that up in front of his own children; apart from being embarrassing, why did he have to bring up the fact that I didn't have a father? But as I drove back home, I reflected on his words. I've never dwelled on my father's death, and in fact, for most of my adult life I have almost insisted that it never happened. As I have related, I denied its impact on me almost from the very day it happened. Mum became such an incredible source of strength to me, moreover, such a powerful and protective figure as she raised her family on her own, that I didn't need to question how I might have been affected. But driving slowly back up the

M1 to Wakefield, I thought: *Uncle is right. If my dad hadn't died, I would probably have followed in his footsteps, begun driving a taxi or maybe had my own restaurant, but I never would have had the ambition I have today. I wouldn't have had to fight for everything; I wouldn't have had that crushing sense that my time on Earth was so limited.*

Now, as I enter the fifth decade of my life and count my many, many blessings, maybe I can finally say that I have grown up along with Penny Appeal. I've accepted my own tragedy, probably in no short measure because I've witnessed so much suffering around the world. Once, on the Turkey/Syria border, we came across refugees who had escaped the most terrifying conflict and the worst human evils: torture, death, rape. Some of them now lived on the street or camped in people's gardens.

They asked me: "Where are you from?" When I told them I was British and lived there, they replied, "Then why are you here?" To them, Britain was a land paved with gold, infused with freedom, redolent of opportunity. Why would someone like me want to leave it, even temporarily, to end up at the edge of a war zone? When I told them that I had come to give them aid from Muslims in the UK, they were brought to tears, shocked, but forever grateful to everyone who had donated and remembered them in a faraway land. I even got messages to take back for the Prime Minister and the Queen – but this Wakefield lad didn't have a means of communicating with either of them directly, so I haven't been able to pass on the messages just yet.

For most of my life, from the age of eight onwards, I never thought of myself as having "old bones". I kept that secret close to my heart for such a long time. I knew, whatever anyone said, that I would follow my father's path at least in one way. It's almost like a betrayal, if I'm honest, losing that secret feeling, as though, somehow, I've pulled away from him. But at the same time, as I move on, I feel his presence increasingly, and that sustains me more than I can say.

Because, of course, there's still so much more to do.

CHAPTER THIRTEEN

SPEEDING FINE

Early in the afternoon of Sunday 29 September, 2019, I was sitting with three Penny Appeal colleagues inside the glistening new Islamabad airport terminal in Pakistan. This trip was the first time I'd been able to use the new terminal – such a powerful symbol of progress in the country. We'd had a successful but exhausting ten days accompanying our two global ambassadors, Mehwish Hayat and James Caan CBE, on a tour of our projects in the Sohawa region, and we'd just said goodbye to everyone there. The air-conditioning was a relief after the 30°-plus dry heat of the countryside. I leaned my head back and gazed up at the sculpted, multicoloured glass installation that covered the huge expanse of ceiling inside the terminal, a cool reference to the truck art of my family's homeland.

What a journey. Ten years earlier, I'd sent off our application to the Charity Commission, with no real idea of how we were going to build an international organisation. Today, over £100 million later, I'd seen through the eyes of our two global ambassadors how the money donated by our supporters in the UK was continuing to change lives for the better in Pakistan. Over ten days, we'd visited several orphan homes, a home for elderly people who had been abandoned by their families, a rural eye camp and a centre for young people. We'd broken ground for a new orphan home complex in Sohawa, as well.

Mehwish and James had been so compassionate and understanding, and had engaged so successfully with the children and the elders and the eye-camp patients; just their presence had brought a sense of hope and optimism to the many people who relied upon our donations to survive in the harsh conditions of rural north-eastern Pakistan. Mehwish is a national superstar, probably the country's most famous and talented actress, the box office queen of Pakistan. Wherever we went, TV cameras followed us to capture every glimpse of her; people flocked to see her, and were amazed by her beauty and sensitivity. James is the international entrepreneur famous for his BBC *Dragons' Den* appearances, and known all over the world for his incisive mind, his debonair TV persona and his impact on business worldwide. Neither of them was the sort to support a charity as a photo op. They both got stuck in, waving away my concerns about their comfort on 4 x 4 journeys across rough terrain. It's not often that I get the chance to stand back and reflect on our work; being with them on this trip had really helped me to see just how powerful Penny Appeal's interventions on the ground had become.

I glanced over at my three team members; they were all sleeping. I closed my eyes as well. We had an hour to go before Flight PK701 took off to fly us back to Manchester. We were all shattered. I couldn't sleep, so I rang Fozia Shah, an executive team member at the Penny Appeal office in Wakefield. I needed to make sure that my car keys would be available at the office when I got back that night; I always left my car there when I took an international flight.

Fozia told me that she'd tried to get into the Penny Appeal office earlier that day, but had been stopped by two private security guards whom she'd never seen before, and who told her that the office was closed. I couldn't figure out what could possibly be happening. What were two private security guards doing there? Penny Appeal didn't employ guards; we were Team Orange, for goodness sake. Who had appointed them? Who was paying for them? Fozia told me that she had rung Samia Hussain, the Director of Operations, to ask what was going on, and from Samia's stuttering response, she realised that her appearance at the Penny Appeal office that Sunday had not been expected – so what was up?

Samia said she would phone Fozia back. She did so a few minutes later, and told her that the building had been closed on account of a gas leak. It all sounded very unlikely

Global Ambassadors, James Caan and Mehwish Hayat
in Pakistan, September 2019

and suspicious to me – surely, if there had been a gas leak, the whole building would be cordoned off. There wouldn't be people standing outside; the whole area would have been cleared. And the police or fire brigade would be there, not two private security guards.

"Fozia," I said. "What is a charity doing employing private security guards? I'm a trustee. I would never approve that kind of expenditure. What's going on?"

Fozia had told me all that she knew. While I was sitting in the airport trying to work it all out, my phone rang again. I pulled it out of my pocket and looked at the screen. It was Ian Wainwright, my fellow Penny Appeal trustee.

"Adeem, it's Ian. Are you on your own?"

I stood up and wandered away from my snoozing colleagues.

"What is it, Ian?"

"Rizwan and I want to meet you at Manchester Airport this evening."

Rizwan, Ian and I were the three trustees of Penny Appeal. Rizwan, as you know, had been with us from the early days, lending his creative genius to our formative strategies. Ian was deeply embedded in Wakefield as the assistant principal of Wakefield College, and he understood very clearly the city that had nurtured me. They were diligent, honourable, trustworthy men.

"You don't need to do that, Ian. It's Sunday night. Spend the evening with your family, we can meet in the office tomorrow."

"It's urgent, Adeem."

"Nothing's that urgent, Ian. It's nice of you to offer, but enjoy your evening and we can talk on Monday morning. We've had a great trip, really successful –"

He interrupted me: "Adeem, we've got to talk. Urgently. Something's happened."

That's when I realised that it was indeed important. "What?"

I replied.

He paused. "I can't say on the phone. We'll see you this evening at the airport."

It's an eight-hour direct flight from Islamabad to Manchester. I hadn't slept much over the previous ten days. Mehwish is a night owl, used to discussing and collaborating into the late hours, and she'd been keen to talk to our local teams as much as she could. James is a morning person, a very focused early riser with meetings booked over breakfast each day. I'd been up early with him each morning too, going over the cost structures of the facilities we were funding, looking at ways of maximising the donors' gifts. I'd been looking forward to some sleep.

Now, with Ian's cryptic phone call swirling around my head, I found myself unable to relax in the cramped confines of the economy seats on Flight PK701. What on Earth could he need to tell me so urgently that couldn't be discussed over the phone?

Over those long hours, as my colleagues caught up on their sleep, I speculated. Penny Appeal has never been a shy organisation. We've never asked for permission or sought to follow the rulebook. As long as projects were being funded and implemented for the good of our beneficiaries, that's all that mattered. Whether you were rich or poor, whatever you could afford we would turn into a transformational activity somewhere in the world. We'd taken that good old Yorkshire saying – *Look after the pennies and the pounds will look after themselves* – and we'd turned it into a global machine to improve millions of people's lives. In ten years, we'd become one of the most successful British Muslim charities, as committed to helping starving children in Somalia as we were to stepping up at home to combat domestic violence or help out at disasters such as Grenfell.

But had I been too quick to shrug off the occasional background gripe? Our foot-to-the-floor approach both to raising funds and distributing them in the field had sometimes caused ripples in the older-charity establishment, but I just thought that came with the territory. I knew that what we were doing in Pakistan, Syria, Ethiopia, Gaza, Yemen, in towns and cities all over the UK, was both vital and effective. Each year, we submitted our detailed annual accounting summary to the Charity Commission, a vital process for every major charity that ensures that an organisation always maintains the highest accounting and reporting standards.

A new image appeared in my mind. I had walked around the Kaaba in Makkah the previous New Year's Eve, clutching the strong arm of Dr Bilal as we completed our *Umrah*. I remembered the confusion I felt, amidst those thousands of other pilgrims, praying to God for guidance on what I should do about my own role at Penny Appeal ten years on from its foundation. Did it still need me? I had found no answer to that question, but now, sitting in this uncomfortable aeroplane, my head was ringing with its significance.

I shifted sleeplessly in my seat as I began to recall the occasional warning from those I considered true friends and family: *Be careful, Adeem: not everyone who smiles to your face means you well. Some people aren't happy about the noise Penny Appeal makes, the waves it causes.* What did they mean? Why wouldn't everyone want to share in the joy of what we'd achieved so far? What could possibly be wrong with fighting to save one more life, one more person's sight, to build one more clean water well, to teach one more orphan to read?

I've never had time for negativity. I never felt there were enough hours in the day to get done the things I wanted to achieve, so why fret about the odd eggshell when you're trying to serve up the world's largest omelette? We'd made the best use of the small change, and we were fulfilling our promise to make a big difference with it. But now I began desperately to think

"I've never had time for negativity. I never felt there were enough hours in the day to get done the things I wanted to achieve."

through everything we'd done. I felt certain that the question I'd asked as we circled the Kaaba was about to be answered.

Finally, at Manchester Airport, I said goodbye and thank you to my colleagues and walked over to meet Rizwan and Ian, who were standing, unsmiling, over to one side.

"Well, guys," I said, "it's got to be something really special to bring you here on a Sunday evening. What's up?" I knew both of them well enough for us to dispense with trivialities. We hugged, as we always did.

Rizwan spoke first. He couldn't have looked more uncomfortable. "Are you all right, Adeem?" he asked gently.

"I haven't slept for forty-eight hours and I've just lost five hours flying back west, so I'm a bit groggy, but guys, I'm always happy to see you. Do you want to tell me what's going on?"

"Let's get a coffee," Ian said.

Over the course of the next three hours, seated amongst the few solitary Sunday-evening coffee drinkers in Caffè Nero, I discovered that my worst fears on the flight back from Islamabad were not without foundation. Following a formal allegation by the then CEO – the Sheikh – Ian and Rizwan, as trustees of Penny Appeal, had felt obliged to submit a Serious Incident Report to the Charity Commission. While that investigation was underway, I had to be suspended with immediate effect from my role as Chair of the trustees.

I'd been fired.

My exhaustion vanished. I knew I had to be clear in my thinking, so I plied the guys with questions, but they weren't able to answer many of them. They handed me an official-looking letter in a sealed envelope, which I shoved in my bag without reading. I kept questioning them and they continued carefully, as they were obliged to, to answer diplomatically and evasively. Neither of them wanted to be in the position they found themselves in, that was obvious. Why would they? They'd been handed a poisoned chalice.

And then I heard my mum's voice in my head: "Adeem ... that's not right, son."

I'd invited her, and other family members, to the party celebrating ten years of Penny Appeal earlier that year. It was a big event, packed with staff and donors and celebrities and media. Dr Hany El-Banna, the founder of Islamic Relief, one of the biggest Islamic charities in the world, did me the honour of giving the keynote address, praising Penny Appeal's work and pledging his support for the future. Despite my fierce focus on the objectives of the charity and the tools we use to maximise potential income for our projects in the field, I never made a point of seeking the limelight. I'm always happy for Penny Appeal to be seen as what it is: an organisation that works because of the commitment of everyone within it. So I'd been happy for the Sheikh to give the main speech of the night, talking about the history of the charity, all that we'd achieved, plans for the future.

Once he'd sat down to a big round of applause, Mum turned to me and said: "Adeem, that man never mentioned you. He made it sound like Penny Appeal was his idea. That's not right, son."

I brushed away her concerns, told her it was fine, I didn't mind the guy taking a bit of credit. After all, I'd given him the job of running the charity four years earlier, as Chief Executive, and he and I had collaborated well. We'd quadrupled our annual income, increased our global impact and were now a major presence at home and abroad. So he wanted to take a little credit? That was OK by me. It was the Penny Appeal way: as long as the projects on the ground were working and growing, as long as the donors were able to see how effectively we were helping our recipients, nothing else mattered.

And it was my way, too, to encourage people, mentor them, push them to achieve their best. This fellow had never been the chief executive of anything before I appointed him, but he seemed to have the will, the energy and the commitment ... so I supported him all the way. So he never invited me into his house? That was OK; not everyone is as sociable as I am. So he seemed to make what were, in my view, poor personnel choices? Well, maybe they'd turn out to be OK. I'd rather give someone a chance than knock them down. And even when the odd rumour came my way, I thought my role was to stand by him. Now, looking back, I can identify a weakness in my leadership approach. I had created Penny Appeal, filled it with my own hope and energy, and I had done everything I could over the years to maximise the charity's ability to raise funds for the needy. And then I had stepped back, allowing an individual to conduct himself in ways that, deep down, I knew were not correct. I criticise myself now for allowing the Sheikh to exercise his authority unchallenged. And it has been one of my personal outcomes of this affair for me to strengthen my leadership approach.

I never minded that the Sheikh had been rewarded for his work at Penny Appeal with an OBE, an honour bestowed on him in January 2019 at Buckingham Palace. I didn't even mind that he had used one or two individuals in our Penny Appeal network to promote his case for receiving the award. *Good for him,* is what I thought. I have to confess, though, that when he informed me he was going to receive the honour because of his charitable work with the Muslim community in his role at Penny Appeal, I didn't want to tell him that I'd never heard of it before. I'm a Wakefield lad, brought up on the Eastmoor council estate. We didn't have many OBEs in our street.

Anyway, he hadn't been the only Penny Appeal staff member to receive such an accolade. In 2019, Tayyebah Jiva was awarded an MBE for her work with vulnerable children over twenty years, in recognition of her work with Penny Appeal. And plenty of other Penny Appeal staff have been honoured over the years for service to their communities and to communities around the world.

We'd all been moving so fast the last four years since the Sheikh had become Chief Executive. Whatever doubts I might have held about the fellow, I always showed him the respect I believed was in order. Unless someone either does their job badly or does something to upset me, I remain supportive.

As I looked at Rizwan's and Ian's sorrowful, serious faces, I felt angry. This man, this chief executive whose job I had given him, and counselled, had broken the Golden Rule of *teamwork making the dream work*. It's cheesy, I know, and you've heard it many times already in this book, but it's true just the same. Penny Appeal only works if all of us – staff, donors, partners, recipients – hold each other tight and embrace the same determined vision.

After a few hours, we'd talked enough. I could see how emotionally drained both of them were, how deeply pained by this awful situation. As we stood up, I hugged them both once more.

"Don't worry, guys," I said. "We'll get through this. We've had challenges before, we'll have challenges in the future. We'll get through it. That's what we always do."

Maybe Rizwan and Ian weren't expecting the optimism, or

hope, or comfort. They'd probably thought they were coming to console *me* somehow.

The M62 was pretty quiet that night as I sat in the back of the car on the way home to Wakefield. My four kids would be asleep by the time I got home; I'd missed their bedtime. Well, I'd see them in the morning. But I was disappointed, and that just stirred the anger inside me further.

There was more drama to come. Late as it was, I phoned my private office, located in the building adjacent to Penny Appeal. As a successful web-based business, it's pretty much a twenty-four-hour operation. To my astonishment, I was told that the Sheikh had gained access to my company's building on Saturday, the evening before, and had removed some of the company's equipment from the secure server vault. He had apparently encouraged a couple of Penny Appeal staff members to accompany him while he took away devices that did *not* belong to the charity. I was shown CCTV footage that quite clearly revealed the Sheikh removing servers and directing others to take equipment from Victoria Chambers late into the evening.

What could this man have been thinking? He had clumsily arranged for the removal of servers, telling the guys removing them that they belonged to the charity. In doing so, he tripped the fibre optic switch that provided the high-speed Internet access on which both the charity and the businesses relied for connectivity. As a result of his staggering own goal, Penny Appeal's Internet didn't function for forty-four days. Forty-four long days, unproductive for nearly 200 employees unable to connect with each other and get online. It was a huge, unprecedented waste of charity resources in every way. This was not only a bad plan, but now the incompetence of its execution had stuck the whole of the charity in darkness for the next month and a half.

Still in the back of the car, my anger rose even more steadily. Now much of it was connected with specific people. I thought of Ali in Rahoon, providing for an entire family and educating the children of my late father's village for £30 a month. I thought of the patient, knowledgeable way he had educated me, all those years ago, about the cycle of poverty. Was Ali to be let down now, if the charity we built by following his example plunged into chaos? I thought about Hassan, the teenager at the eye camp who wept when he discovered that his sight might have been saved six weeks earlier. Didn't our responsibilities lie with people in his position, all over the world? What value did our egos have in comparison with that duty?

I thought of some of the towers of strength who had built Penny Appeal with me, huge characters like Haroom Mota, our Head of Challenges, who had raised enormous sums of money through his arduous marathons, and who had personally motivated me to run three marathons myself in aid of the charity. How could I look people like him in the eye if all of this was for nothing? I thought of Saadia Shamali, the brave, entrepreneurial mother of five who just needed a helping hand to get sufficient irrigation going on her plot of land in Gaza. Were we honouring her by *squabbling*, back here in Yorkshire?

But I wasn't squabbling. I hadn't squabbled with anyone, in fact. This disaster had all been created by one rogue element. Once more, my thoughts turned back to the *Umrah*. Was this the answer I had sought? Was I now being challenged? Was this the moment when I said, "OK, I'll walk away, I'll let you all take care of Penny Appeal and I wish you good fortune in your endeavours?" Or was this the moment for me to say, *I understand: my work isn't done. Vulnerable people around the world still need help. There is more for me to do, to enable Penny Appeal to realise its true potential. We could now, at this ten-year point, be just at the start of an incredible journey.*

During that car journey, I reflected long and hard on the responsibility which I felt for allowing this beautiful charity to be so endangered by one man. And I promised myself that, if I got through this, I would never again let Penny Appeal fall prey to one individual's ego.

Abdul Wahab, the Penny Appeal colleague who had come to pick me up, interrupted my thoughts. Like Rizwan and Ian, he seemed on edge. "Er, Adeem," he said. "I had a message. From the Chief Executive. He wants me to drive you straight to his house for a meeting tonight."

The final jigsaw piece fell into place. Now I understood what those two private security guards were doing outside the office; I understood who had authorised their employment – using charity funds. This guy thought he had it all sewn up. He must have thought he had the whole senior leadership team on board for what felt like an attempted coup, which I suspected he'd been preparing for some time. He'd used Penny Appeal lawyers to approve his actions and to draft my suspension letter, and had briefed the international Penny Appeal CEOs against me; he'd even changed all the passwords on the social media accounts, so that I was digitally as well as physically locked out.

And now he seriously expected me to turn up at his house late on a Sunday night, after flying eight hours back from Pakistan? He was probably sitting there, waiting to explain to me how it was all over, how he'd got the other trustees to file a Serious Incident Report with the Charity Commission, how maybe the best thing for all concerned would be for me to offer my resignation. I could almost hear him saying the words, and was left feeling like a player in a scene abandoned on the cutting room floor of *The Godfather*. Did he really think I was going to let this beautiful charity, which I had formed in my father's name and dedicated my entire adult life to building, be taken over and destroyed by one individual's ego?

I shook my head in the dark. "You're OK, Abdul Wahab," I said. "Just take me home please."

We drove in silence back to Wakefield, the city that will always be home to me. I finally felt calm. I was going home.

Reflecting on all this now, eighteen months on, has helped me put into perspective the events of 2019: the whistle-blowing and attempted coup by the Sheikh; the accusations made against me that I knew to be false, but which took an independent enquiry to prove; the turbulence that this entirely unnecessary situation created for our charity, our donors and our recipients. It felt like receiving a speeding fine. I had believed for so long that I would only have a short time in which to get everything done, so perhaps I pushed too hard sometimes, demanded too much, expected others to keep up with the pace I insisted on. But if I hadn't, would we really have helped millions of people around the world?

All the same, when you get a speeding fine, you accept it; you take the speed-awareness course, learn its lessons and continue onwards. So what did I learn? What did we learn at Penny Appeal?

Well, first, the Sheikh resigned from Penny Appeal three months after the night my plane touched down at Manchester Airport. It won't come as much of a surprise to hear that a good number of unsavoury facts came to light in the run-up to his resignation. During those three months, the two guards he'd put in place to block my entry to Penny Appeal remained in place. Can you imagine? Hired muscle standing on the steps every day. I made a point of walking by each day from my Single Muslim office and chatting with them, bringing them coffees to keep warm. We developed a good relationship. Their names were Hafiz and Shoaib. They were just paid to do a job, and I wouldn't try to make their job any more difficult by attempting to enter the building; but I wanted to retain the generosity of spirit that our charity was founded on, and somehow putting my arms around these two strong fellows every day kept the love intact. I travelled around the country, visiting friends of the charity, donors, partners, always reassuring them that this horrible situation would only be temporary, that they shouldn't worry – we would be back in stronger shape than ever before, and soon.

A month after the Sheikh bolted, the independent investigation that was conducted reported to the Charity Commission that there was no evidence in support of any of his numerous and outrageous allegations. On 26 June 2020, the Board reconvened and I was finally reinstated – after a struggle, damage to my reputation and financial loss to the charity – as a trustee of Penny Appeal. It's hard to put into words what I went through during those months, opening up my life, my personal records, everything to the lawyers, auditors and investigators. I did it because I knew that the truth would out, however painful it was for me and for my family to be subjected to such an ordeal.

Have a quick look at the front cover of this book. It looks like I'm standing in front of something very orange – very Penny Appeal orange. In fact, the photograph was taken by a good friend of mine on 5 November 2019 at the Tate Gallery in London. The backdrop is a 1993 artwork by Rudolf Stingel, for which he covered an entire wall with bright orange carpet, allowing viewers to go up and create patterns in it with their hands. The idea, I think, is to allow museum-goers to feel that they are intrinsically involved in the art. I'd come down to London for a couple of days to meet up with two old friends. We three lads were just going to meet up, make each other laugh and generally catch up. It had been a few weeks since my suspension was announced, and I really felt the need to spend some time with people I trusted, to get out of Wakefield just for a short break. The pressure was really on: I felt like the world was looking at me in a different way, that those wild and untrue allegations were eroding all the achievements I'd made in my life to that point. I was feeling very raw, lonely and – unusually, for me – quite vulnerable. The coup attempt had shaken me. It hadn't shaken my belief in myself or in Penny Appeal, but it had caused me untold amounts of pain.

My friends had suggested that we met at the Tate. It's one of the places I love to visit in London, and I always find something to take away in mind, something to inspire me. But I wasn't expecting Rudolf Stingel's artwork: we turned the corner, and there it was, this massive orange wall. I was speechless. My friends started to laugh.

"There you go, Adeem," one said. "Now, what's that saying to you?"

I couldn't put it into words. But somehow I knew what it meant, and in a way its impact was, I hope, an expression of what Stingel was trying to achieve, because in that instant, I knew that our big orange charity was going to come through this challenge. I knew we were going to emerge from this upheaval stronger, more powerful, more effective, more able to help than ever before. I now had a clear answer to my prayers on New Year's Eve. I knew where my future lay. It was a defining moment for me, and that, I think, explains the big grin on my face.

The one thing that had sustained me since my return was prayer. Like many believers, I find that the daily demands of work and family can intrude upon my prayers. I suspect my prayers can become mechanical when my head is filled with other pressing concerns. You get down on the mat and, instead of focusing everything on your devotion to the Creator of the universe, you find yourself worrying about when an Amazon delivery is going to

"As I prayed in the days and weeks that followed my suspension, I found that I was praying so hard that I could actually taste the sweetness of each word I was saying."

be made, or why the WiFi is running slowly. But as I prayed in the days and weeks that followed my suspension, I found that I was praying so hard that I could actually taste the sweetness of each word I was saying, thanking the Almighty for all the blessings and for the support of old and new friends. I was regularly in tears on the prayer mat. Of course, I was praying to find a way to get out of that turbulence, to find a dignified solution. But it was also true that one of the blessings resulting from the attempted coup was the opportunity God gave me to really connect with Him in a way that one often doesn't on a daily basis. I genuinely felt in awe of God's greatness, His might, and of how we are in control of nothing, of how insignificant we are. I really love the fact that God had put me in that position, that He allowed me truly to experience prayer, to feel its power. And I felt entirely humble that I had now been given the opportunity to experience certainty about my confusion in Makkah a year earlier.

A passage in the Qur'an holds that after hardship will come ease; now, a year or so later, I'm starting to feel some of that ease. As Muslims, we believe that a hard life will lead to a comfortable grave, that hardship will one day be relieved – if not in this life, then in the afterlife. Hardship can be unbearable; you start to believe it is never going to end. And that is when faith teaches us that we have in fact been blessed: the hardship is a gift of understanding.

Each day, as I prayed, I learned to remember what was important: to honour my mother and take good care of her; to do whatever I could to help others; and above all, to remember to stay as close to God as I could. I had the good fortune to feel my connection to God more strongly than ever during those months, and that understanding will never leave me. For that, I shall always be grateful.

Spiritual awareness was the most important lesson of this whole period. But there were others. Without wanting to rake up too much depressing detail, the Sheikh's senior position had obliged my fellow trustees to take his allegations seriously, though I knew they were outrageous. That's why they commissioned the independent investigation that cleared me. No one who really knew me believed the allegations for a second, but what about other people – journalists, commentators, people who hadn't liked seeing me succeed in business? These ghastly accusations could have a serious impact on my reputation and, were it not for the fact that the investigation was quick to clear my name, I could have suffered a permanent injury to my standing.

People I love have warned me to be more careful about trusting others. But I'm not so sure; part of me still believes that you should extend as much trust as you can, that only by being completely trusting can you bring out the best in most people, help them flourish. It's only a small minority that uses it against you: the one in ten. At the same time, having now experienced the damage that can be wreaked by the one in ten, I must admit I am determined never to allow such an individual to operate wrongfully with such freedom ever again.

For Penny Appeal, the outcome has been extremely

beneficial. Not only has a bad apple been rooted out – we have also been given the opportunity to strengthen our organisation across the board. We have a new management team in place headed up by Harris Iqbal as Interim Chief Executive. (Harris was previously Penny Appeal's Director of International Programmes.) And reminiscent of the way in which Rizwan and I set out the fundamentals of the organisation back in 2012, we have collectively agreed on a set of character definitions for Penny Appeal that will carry us through the next ten years of our progress. We know who we are: a British Muslim humanitarian and development relief organisation that operates worldwide, rooted deeply in Islamic traditions. We know what we still believe in: reward and affordability, providing our donors with a full range of giving opportunities for a minimum of a few pennies – because we know from more than a decade's worth of experience that a pocketful of pennies can transform worlds. And because every one of our relief programmes is steeped in Islamic beliefs, giving even a few pennies constitutes an act of faith for our donors – and with it, therefore, spiritual rewards according to the guidance of the Qur'an.

We are maintaining and strengthening the characteristics that have so far defined us. We are proud of our Yorkshire roots, and are about to begin a whole new era, with a new headquarters in our home city of Wakefield. We still consider ourselves to be "the People's Charity", defined by our close and responsive relationship with our donors. As soon as the Covid-19 threat begins to diminish, we shall return to staging live events across the country, reinforcing our message of affordable and effective giving. We shall stay noisy! Nobody ever changed the world for the good by hiding away and being silent. We'll continue to do what we've always done, in our bright orange T-shirts: get out and about, talk to people, help people, be active, be the first to offer assistance. We'll keep increasing the charitable work we undertake at home here in Britain as long as our donors keep reminding us of the work that needs to be done.

We shall continue our partnerships with proven organisations around the world to allocate donors' funds, increasing the abilities of our partners to deliver our programmes: OrphanKind, Hifz Orphan, Mosque Project, Education First, Thirst Relief, Feed Our World. These programmes were created years ago, specifically to bring donors and recipients together in a spiritually rewarding relationship, and they grow stronger and more productive each year. Moreover, in 2020 we began committing ourselves to expanding all of them significantly. That will require us to carry on growing our donor income through a continuous annual programme of events and campaigns whereby we can present the needs of developing countries to our communities. It will encourage us to deepen our relationships with donors, so that they always feel reassured that their charitable giving has been used effectively.

Ever since we took the decision to look after those five little girls in Sohawa in 2007 and received safeguarding training from SOS Villages in Islamabad, we have always been entirely committed to the welfare of our recipients, young and old. We have responsibilities towards people of all ages in over thirty countries around the world, and I am proud of our record in upholding the highest standards of safeguarding everywhere we work. However, as with almost all major global charities, there can be instances where delivery falls short of expectations, and on the rare occasions when that happens, we act very swiftly.

In August 2020, we were alerted to serious safeguarding allegations involving our OrphanKind work in The Gambia. In 2018, after three years of building and a seven-figure donor investment, we opened the state-of-the-art Medina Orphan Village in Yarambamba. The Medina contained ten orphan homes with capacity for ten residents each, thus reaching a maximum occupancy of 100 vulnerable children at any given time. Each home had a dedicated foster mother who was trained to care for the children as if they were her own. The eco-friendly, secure complex was built to the highest possible standards, with solar power for light, heating and cooling. The Medina also contained a mosque, herb garden, medical clinic, outdoor play yard and an admin block that served as a hub for Penny Appeal's extensive West Africa development portfolio.

We opened The Medina with former world-champion boxer Amir Khan, whose personal foundation was a big supporter of the project. Amir had been as convinced as I was by the original proposal back in 2014. As mentioned earlier, the Sheikh – newly appointed as Penny Appeal's CEO – had suggested that we look at The Gambia as part of our expansion into other countries where increased donor income could be used. His recommendation made sense: The Gambia is one of the world's poorest nations, ranking 172 out of 189 countries according to the 2020 Human Development Index. Approximately three-quarters of the rural population is classified as "poor" or "extremely poor". In 2014, the Sheikh's personal contact in The Gambia, Atabou Aidara, was involved with an NGO there, and the Sheikh assured us that he was the man to lead the project. In due course, Atabou was appointed CEO of Penny Appeal Gambia, and set about building The Medina with our donors' money.

When the safeguarding alert dropped like a bombshell in August 2020, it was hugely distressing for us all. It made me sick to my core to think that children for whom we were responsible could have been mistreated. It went against everything I've ever stood for. Online rumours spread about allegations of criminal, unsafe actions in The Gambia, but it was very difficult for us to find out what was true and what was false. Our responsibility for the children was paramount, though. Harris Iqbal knew the Gambia setup well from his previous position directing our international programmes, and was quick to take action, immediately withdrawing the children concerned from the homes and appointing a separate international agency to investigate the claims of abuse, working closely with the Gambian government and the UK Charity Commission. The investigation is still underway as I write this, so I am unable to comment further; but I am proud of the way Harris and his team have tackled the issue directly – the wellbeing of the children themselves are the team's absolute priority. Harris has not only responded so quickly in The Gambia itself, but has gone one step further, arranging an independent root-and-branch review of safeguarding arrangements across Penny Appeal, including a fresh look at our policies. He has quadrupled the resources allocated to safeguarding globally, and once again demonstrated that we are always on the side of the vulnerable wherever we work.

Until the investigation concludes, we simply do not know the facts of the matter: what actually occurred, which safeguards failed and which succeeded. Once there are lessons to be learned, they shall be implemented. We suffered a failure of trust by encouraging the Sheikh to promote his contact to run the orphan complex, and believed that all our strict safeguarding guidelines were being followed. But we are mature organisation, and we will take responsibility for any and all shortcomings. It's the right thing to do even though the allegations centre around downstream partners ADD, at least twice removed from our UK teams. We can never allow anything like this to be remotely possible on our watch and will do everything we can to ensure our work is conducted with the highest safety provisions in place.

○

The Gambia crisis was a second 'speeding fine' – another warning for us. Penny Appeal has, without a doubt, emerged from these recent difficulties as a far stronger, more closely bonded organisation, ready to continue its growth from our new headquarters. The Qur'an says: "Whoever saves a life, it is as if he has saved the whole of mankind." That is the abiding spirit of Penny Appeal, and always shall be.

The eighteen months or so that followed the attempted coup by the Sheikh in September 2019 have been the most challenging time for everyone at Penny Appeal. Harris has done a phenomenal job as our interim CEO. He is, perhaps, the youngest person in the country in such a role, and yet he has handled the leadership transition like an old pro. In true Penny Appeal spirit, he has got on with the job, fending off rumours and social media backlash, and just doing whatever has needed to be done. The year 2020 was a difficult one for most charities; thousands of them simply did not survive the financial crunch that the pandemic brought. The newly formed Penny Appeal Executive Board acted early and decisively, pivoting to work-from-home during the first lockdown and reviewing all our programme commitments, given the increased risk Covid-19 presented. By the time Ramadan 2020 was over – a Holy Month unlike any we have experienced – Harris and the new team had been able to make millions of pounds of cost-cutting reforms, marking a firm shift away from many of the Sheikh's status projects. Perhaps most remarkable is that despite the virus and the leadership transition, the new team increased our income over 30 per cent compared to the previous year!

Adeem speaking at the Sohawa Complex, Pakistan, September 2019

The team has also risen to the challenge of responding to the Gambia crisis in a diligent, compassionate and professional manner. While the final outcome is still to be determined, I am humbled by the decisive action and leadership demonstrated by Harris and the whole organisation. Now, as we start to build towards a "new normal", I want to take a moment to acknowledge the incredible team that has been with us in this testing time. Those eighteen months were also the toughest of my colleagues' professional lives, but they pulled together in a phenomenal way, maintaining their productivity and working tirelessly on behalf of those around the world who are most vulnerable. When the Gambia news broke, the emotional weight of the allegations weighed down on us all. It forced us to question everything. Yet we soldiered on and did the right thing by those we seek to serve, reforming and levelling up every dimension of our safeguarding. I am truly honoured to have each and every person at Penny Appeal by my side.

We have also approved the appointment of two world-leading organisations to conduct a full review following this incident. Penny Appeal invited Barnardo's to conduct a root-and-branch review of safeguarding arrangements across the organisation, covering all areas of operations. And Keeping Children Safe, an expert safeguarding agency, was commissioned to conduct an independent investigation into the allegations coming from The Gambia.

Personally, I feel that I have emerged from this period as a stronger person, and am perhaps readier now than ever before in my life to accept and discuss the impact upon me of the loss of my father at such an early age. I honour my beloved Mum, who still keeps me in line from that very same house in Wakefield, the front door of which became such a boundary for me as a child. Now with four beautiful children of my own, I am proud of the connections within my own family, back to Mum and Dad, my two sisters and their families, to Grandad, to our wider family in the UK and Pakistan. I have clarity, calm and purpose – a far cry from the confused thirty-eight-year-old circling the Kaaba on New Year's Eve two years ago. For the gift of such certainty, I shall remain grateful for the rest of my life.

CHAPTER FOURTEEN

LOOKING TO THE FUTURE

It seems fitting that as I come to the end of this book, New Year's Eve, December 2020, is only a day or two away. The unprecedented events of 2020 – or, at least, the worst of them – shall hopefully be behind us all soon, allowing us to gather once more to continue planning our future. For Penny Appeal, the move to our very own premises in the heart of Wakefield in 2021 will be a significant change.

Five years ago, I was persuaded that Penny Appeal needed to inhabit its own office space, separate from Single Muslim's offices around the corner. I understood the logic, and as a businessman, I knew that poor working conditions can slow people down unnecessarily. Over the next few years, we just got busier, too, building more call-centre rooms, bringing in additional programme experts to manage projects. We went from £10 million a year to £30 million. Each time the charity grew in scope, we would lease more rooms from our office-block landlords. The building wasn't really set up for one organisation, so we ended up with a warren of rooms on different floors with no central meeting space. It was becoming difficult to foster a sense of unity. Penny Appeal's unbridled energy and enthusiasm were being stifled by the rigid layout and the jumble of rooms we occupied. In addition, we had an inbuilt potential weakness: what if the landlord decided to sell the building? How disruptive would it be to Penny Appeal's work to have to make a fast, unplanned move?

There was another factor. Our donors had encouraged us to look at doing more humanitarian work here in the UK, and we needed to take a good look at how we reflected our values accurately, and to display our growing commitment to working with the vulnerable in Britain. We needed to buy Penny Appeal its own home – a place where we could work together as we needed to, plan our continued growth, invite people in with pride to work alongside us, contribute ideas, add to the energy

Penny Appeal global family in Wakefield, 2020

of the charity. Penny Appeal plans to be a permanent feature of both the international charity landscape and its home city of Wakefield. We now needed to reflect that maturity by having a permanent place to live and work. Our ambition at Penny Appeal is to make Wakefield a significant player in the international humanitarian landscape, and our new HQ is the next step towards realising that vision.

We haven't reached the point we're at by chance or luck. We have been able to honour the charitable wishes of our donors by putting in hard, dedicated work. As a team, we have achieved an astounding amount: success comes when people are organised, motivated, skilled and passionate. Having proved ourselves in this way, we can also help other, younger organisations to reach their own potential, to show them what we have done, how we operate, to motivate and encourage them to follow in our steps. For these reasons, too – the desire to be of service to others – we need our own proper public building into which to invite the community.

This is where I need to take you back in time again.

I'm sixteen years old and sitting in the design classroom of Wakefield College. Most of the teachers at the college aren't particularly interested in me: I don't perform well in Maths or English or Science, and can't seem to focus on detail. My mind is always buzzing with the little schemes I've got going; college education somehow seems too dry, divorced from the busy life I've got outside the classroom. But the two teachers of my graphic design course, Tony and Ron, are different: they talk directly to me, tell me I've got potential. Theirs is the only class, if I'm honest, where I pay attention. For some reason, these two lovely fellows spied some potential in this daydreaming

"As a team, we have achieved an astounding amount: success comes when people are organised, motivated, skilled and passionate."

boy, and they both pushed me to work harder at design – which I did.

When the opportunity came up for a work placement, they rewarded me by sending me off to work at the ITV studios in Leeds, rather than posting me to some bland office where I'd be stuck in a back room doing photocopying. As you already know, my brief time at ITV was revelatory, and filled me with an ambition to *create* that remains to this day. If Tony and Ron hadn't taken a kindly interest in me, I'd have never built Single Muslim; as a consequence, I would never have been in a position to start up Penny Appeal and to help make it the success it has become.

In the years after I left college, I'd occasionally bump into either Tony or Ron in Wakefield, and they always asked with genuine interest how I was doing. As my business became successful, they even invited me back to the college to give talks to the students, which I did. I remember scouring my young audience, trying to find someone like me who just needed some encouragement to make a success of his or her life. Those occasions were very special to me.

The rooms where I studied were in a grand collection of buildings in Thornes Park, in the centre of Wakefield, and once housed an old school called Thornes House High School, which

Acquiring Thornes Park Campus, November 2018, Adeem with Wakefield College principal Sam Wright

opened in 1921. It came under the wing of Wakefield College in 1993, just before I attended. It was mostly arts that were taught in this part of the College – performing arts, music, fine arts, design, media – but business studies and sport were also taught there during my time as a student.

The buildings are tucked away in the heart of Thornes Park, surrounded by trees. Just to the north, within the confines of the park still, is the city's main athletics stadium, next door to a more recent skatepark. Elsewhere, there are acres of green fields and trees. The park is the most important bit of greenery in the centre of Wakefield. It's loved by dog walkers, runners, families, sporty girls and boys. If I exit my Single Muslim offices in Victoria Chambers, bang in the centre of Wakefield, I can walk to Thornes Park within twenty minutes.

That's exactly what I plan to be doing in 2021. Nearly three years ago, a friend alerted me to the fact that a proposed sale of Wakefield College's Thornes Park campus had fallen through. The college had decided to sell the buildings and move many of the arts courses into its Margaret Street campus, in the city centre. The final classes were going to be given in Thornes Park in 2019, and then the buildings would be handed over to the acquiring party, a housing development. But in 2018, this proposed sale collapsed, and the college sought another buyer.

It didn't take me long to realise that this was the perfect solution to Penny Appeal's need for a permanent home, and a symbolic one. I am a product of Wakefield College, and so proud of my home city ... what could be more appropriate?

By the time we came to look at it with serious intent, in 2018, the Thornes Park buildings had seen better days. The paint was flaking, there were tiles missing on some of the roofs, here and there the odd gate hung on one hinge. Times have been hard for educational establishments such as Wakefield College. They simply didn't have the funds to keep the buildings in top condition. The campus had become a rather sad, neglected quarter of our city.

My fellow trustees and I pored over the details, and decided to make an offer for the whole Thornes Park campus, which would give Penny Appeal a permanent physical home big enough to allow us to continue growing and to reach out to groups, individuals and businesses in Wakefield that needed help. The price we offered would allow us to refurbish the buildings and still end up with a cost-effective, long-term base for the charity. For me, it would be a dream come true; for the charity, it would be our first genuine symbol of permanence.

And so it was. Were it not for the unexpected impact of Covid-19, we would have moved into Thornes Park already – but we shall hopefully begin moving our staff, many of whom have been working from home during the pandemic, into their new home from the middle of 2021.

There are many benefits for Penny Appeal in the new place. For a start, we shall have plenty of outdoor space in which to host a permanent soup kitchen. The old college had a large canteen with appropriate cooking facilities, so we'll also be able to invite homeless people in Wakefield in to be fed. Our kitchen will provide meals to the elderly as well. We'll have assembly rooms in which to host community events. There is a 180-seat theatre there, which we can use for fundraising events, and we can make it available to other community and arts groups as well. There's a swimming pool that can be used for community activities, and a sports hall that our staff can use as a gym – but which we can also make available to the community. Thornes Park can become a vital hub in Wakefield, a place where people of all backgrounds can come together, infused with the value of respect for one another. We're already talking to a wide variety of groups, from the Wakefield Wildcats rugby club to the Bishop of Wakefield – all of whom have said they would welcome being

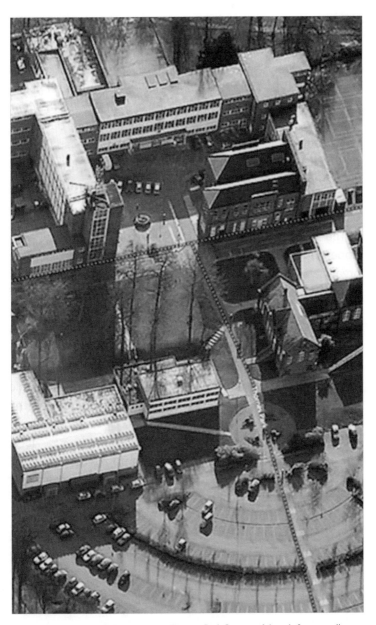

Penny Appeal's new Wakefield home at Thornes Park Campus, Adeem's former college

able to share the space with us.

Penny Appeal can thus give back to the city that first welcomed it, and have a positive impact to counter Wakefield's recent history of civic decline. We shall provide jobs for young people; our call centre there will be a place where they can learn the same skills I learned when I worked in one during my youth, and while they acquire life skills as well as an income, they will be helping Penny Appeal continue its good works. We'll provide space for organisations such as the Citizens Advice Bureau, too, and maintain drop-in facilities for homeless people in need of help.

The Thornes Park headquarters, like everything else Penny Appeal does, will be a UK first: an example of how a charitable organisation can reach out to individuals, community groups and businesses alike to provide a hub alongside the work of its staff. Often, community centres are funded by national or local governments, and their fortunes depend on the continuation of those funds. With Thornes Park, our embrace of the community will be permanent, because it will become a core element of our forward-looking strategy. Local people have always supported Penny Appeal, and will now see the circle completed: from raising funds to support international projects, then national British projects ... and now local Wakefield projects. This is fundamental to our vision. It will allow our staff to gain a daily understanding of the importance of humanitarian work, and will place us centrally as a Muslim charity in a multi-faith community.

I couldn't be more excited about it all. The new premises and projects will serve as models for the next generation, showing everyone that it is possible, with intention, to work together and build a better, safer, more inclusive community.

"I couldn't be more excited about it all. The new premises and projects will serve as models for the next generation."

CHAPTER FIFTEEN

A BRITISH MUSLIM STORY

There's always a new way to look at things. To mark the tenth anniversary of Penny Appeal's foundation, we decided to hand over the reins to the next generation. It seemed appropriate: we wanted an unusual way to register the fact that we'd been operating for a decade, and we've always been a youthful charity. What better way to commemorate than by inviting a ten-year-old British child to come in and take charge?

Ten-year-old Shakira was appointed "Kid Boss" of Penny Appeal in 2019, with a remit to come in, chair meetings and give us – ten years into our own journey – a feel for how the young people of this country view the issues facing the world. She was refreshing: direct, funny, thoughtful and full of ideas. At one of the early meetings, she decided to bring in a kids' toy called Slime to get us all to relax before talking business. I still remember the fun we had smearing this disgusting stuff all over the Penny Appeal boardroom table.

But there were serious times there, too, and when we took Shakira to visit one of our orphan homes in The Gambia, *she* showed *us* the importance of what we were trying to do. She and the children in the village we visited got on instantly, as though they had grown up together. They chatted about pop stars and games, and shared what they each liked to do with their time. From that experience, we acquired a better understanding of how children see the world, what they want from it – and what they want to see changed. We finished our tenth year with our Kid Boss knowing more about what we have to do to respond to the ideals and desires of the generation coming along behind us.

Perhaps we'll invite Shakira back in 2029 to take the helm again, when she and we are twenty years old. We'll be able to talk about what we've achieved since 2019, hopefully having helped more people than ever before. And we can make plans then for the third decade.

Looking at things in a different way: that has always been the Penny Appeal approach. In 2018 we won the Creative Media Award for our campaign *As British As A Cup Of Tea*, which we featured over the festive period in December 2017 on ITV, Channel Five and the London Underground. The campaign was designed to illustrate how our Muslim faith comes from the East, but at the same time we are proudly British, working around the world but also here at home in the UK.

Today is 28 December 2020. Looking out my window here in Wakefield, I see frost on the cars. They're forecasting heavy snow tonight, and two lanes of the M6 over towards Manchester are already closed, with reports of cars being abandoned. Storm Bella, that's the name they've given to this latest bout of nasty weather. I'll have to remember my Wellington boots when I go out with the children later.

Meanwhile, in the Khyber Pakhtunkhwa region of north-west Pakistan, families are preparing for the big freeze that comes every few years as a result of La Niña, the weather pattern that causes colder ocean temperatures in the Pacific. These families have only just got through the flooding that hit their region in August, and they're also struggling to protect themselves from the coronavirus pandemic now sweeping through Pakistan. Without help, thousands of people there could die from the cold season. The same situation faces the 3.6 million internally displaced people in Yemen, many of whom are living in makeshift shelters as the cold weather arrives; again, without help, they won't survive it. In Palestine, Covid-19 has had a terrible impact on the 53 per cent of the population living in poverty. Children are running about throughout the Gaza Strip without the warm clothing they will

"Eleven years on from its foundation, Penny Appeal still has a lot to do."

need to protect themselves from hypothermia this coming winter. In Afghanistan's Parwan Province, where August floods killed over 500 people and destroyed over 1,500 homes, many families won't even have temporary shelters in which to shield themselves from the snow – which is on its way. And all around us here in the UK, 320,000 homeless people will be facing life-threatening temperatures on the streets in the coming weeks if they can't find support and assistance.

Eleven years on from its foundation, Penny Appeal still has a lot to do. Right now, we have people at the end of the phone lines, accepting small donations. As part of our Winter Emergency Appeal, for as little as £25, donors can protect some of the people I've just mentioned by funding food packs, hygiene kits, warm blankets, clothing, fuel, shelters. We're still making charity around the world both affordable and rewarding. Nothing's changed on that front.

As ever, we're not standing still. We're going to see much of our hard work over the last ten years start to pay dividends. The international offices will really begin to step up and make serious contributions to the funding of our programmes. As the People's Charity, we'll become more widespread in our activities here in the UK. We're not the new kid on the block anymore, and in the coming years we'll team up more with governments and major institutions to deliver still more international programmes, as our donors continue to increase their giving. We'll be getting involved in discussions at higher levels about how to take strategic action in different parts of the world.

Having become recognised as a powerful British Muslim asset, we're going to keep demonstrating how Muslims work alongside other faiths for the good of humanity. We're part of the landscape of giving in this country now. Take away the Muslim element, and it makes no sense; take away the British element, that makes no sense, either. Penny Appeal is part of the fabric of millions of people's lives now, both in the UK and around the world, and the knowledge of that fact keeps me focused. Great Britain is made up of many communities, and the way we coexist and support one another makes Britain great. As British Muslims, we represent one such community, and I feel very strongly that we are closely tied to all the others.

From our successes and our mistakes, we've grown smarter, wiser, sharper. After everything we've been through, I am personally committed to making sure that we combine our maturity with the same entrepreneurial hunger we've always had, to bring about a better world. We're not going to become a monolithic, layered organisation; we're going to stay flat, nimble, quick. And we'll maintain complete dedication to the wishes of our donors, because without them, we're nothing. Penny Appeal only ever was, and only ever will be, a tool for our donors to engage with worthy recipients they have a desire to help.

Penny Appeal's recent challenges – the attempted coup and the crisis in our Gambian orphan homes – have made us stronger than ever. We have directly addressed the internal weaknesses that created the conditions for both these situations to occur, and we have recommitted ourselves as an entire organisation to the faith-led principles behind what we do and what our donors want us to do. As this book went to press in late February 2021, we received confirmation from the government in The Gambia that Penny Appeal has been

Covid Emergency Relief in Syrian camps, 2020

approved to reopen its orphan homes there. We will use this period to do what we have always done at Penny Appeal; learn, improve and work tirelessly for those who need our support.

As Talal Al Murad said: *I build people. People build me. We are a team.*

○

And me? I've discovered quite a few things over the past eighteen months, which I never really recognised or faced up to. Perhaps the higher you aim, the bigger and more interesting your challenges become. There never seemed to be any time to 'waste' on self-reflection; I had to keep the pace up, keep racing forward. Now, like many people, I've learned not just from the difficult problems presented in my own life, but from the challenges we have all faced during the pandemic. Prayer has sustained me, and I've reflected on the intimacy with God that this tradition of ours affords us. I've also been reminded of the importance of remaining close to family at all times. The beauty and mystery of the world Allah has created are more real than ever to me now. I see the answer to my prayer in Makkah. I see how God put me through something traumatic for me to find a renewed sense of purpose, to fight to be where I am. Sometimes God isolates us from each other in order to connect us to Him, and puts us through difficult times in order to strengthen us and remind us who is ultimately in charge. I hold these truths closer to my heart than ever before, and pray these insights can continue to shape my future, and the futures of my family and of Penny Appeal.

Thank you for going on this journey with me. I have one final request (we're never shy to keep asking at Penny Appeal!), and that is that you send us a prayer. Pray for the success of our work, for us to continue to be able to reach more people and lift them out of poverty. Pray also for the hero behind it all: my amazing mother, who has stood by me, never asking for anything, always ready to give. Lastly, pray for my dad. My memories of him are weak, but I hope the legacy we leave in his name is strong, and that he is proud of his boy, who's grown into a man with a family all of his own. The number of years I had with him was small, but they made a big difference to me.

My prayer for you, reader, is that our journey can inspire you to make the small changes you need in your own life that will one day amount to a big difference. Finally, I invite you to join Team Orange. Get involved. Get in touch. Spread the word. We're all in this struggle together, and we can't wait to have you along for the ride.

"The beauty and mystery of the world Allah has created are more real than ever to me now."

Supporting the Mayor of London with the Eid in Trafalgar Square, London 2019

APPENDICES

Appendix One: Our Programme Partners

International

International Partnership	Countries of Operation
ACA (Awareness & Consolation Association)	Lebanon
ACRE (Alliance with Communities for Rural Engagement	DRC/ Uganda/ Zambia
ActionAid	Bangladesh / Palestine / Uganda/ Philippines/ Somaliland
ADT (African Development Trust)	Somalia/ Djibouti/ Sierra Leone/ Kenya/ Eritrea
Afghanistan & Central Asian Association (ACAA)	Afghanistan
Agrajattra	Bangladesh
AITAM	Bangladesh
Al Rowwad Cultural and Arts Society	Palestine
Al-Hikma Foundation	Sri Lanka
Al-Mustafa Trust International	Nepal/Sudan
ALM (Al-Mustafa Lil Umooma Wa Riaayt AL-Tifl)	Sudan / Niger
AMRF (Arsenic Mitigation and Research Foundation)	Bangladesh
Amurtel	Greece
Annasru Deen & Development	Senegal/ Mauritania/ Sierra Leone/ Nigeria/ Niger/ Mali/ Guinea Bissau/ Guinea/ Mauritania
Ar-rehma Trust	Tanzania
Beyaz Eller	Syria
CanDo	Syria
Collateral Repair Project	Jordan
Concern Worldwide	Bangladesh / Somalia / Kenya
DAM (Dhaka Ahsania Mission)	Bangladesh

Friends of the Blind Association	Palestine
FRO (Friends of Orphans)	Uganda
Global One	Bangladesh / Nigeria
GlobalMedic	India / Indonesia / Syria
Good Works Studio	Bangladesh
GWQ (Generations without Qat for Awareness & development)	Yemen
HAWCA (Humanitarian Assistance for the Women and Children of Afghanistan)	Afghanistan
HELP (Health, Education & Literary Programme)	Pakistan
Human Appeal International	Palestine/ Azerbaijan
Human Care	Syria
Human Concern	Syria
Human Relief Foundation	Iraq
IBC (International Blue Crescent)	Somalia/ Turkey/ Syria
IDEA	Bangladesh
IGSSS (Indo-Global Social Service Society)	India
ILM (International Learning Movement)	India/UK
Insan	Lebanon
Interpal	Palestine
IRC (International Rescue Committee)	Lebanon, Bangladesh
Islamic Help	CAR/ Cameroon/ Bosnia/ Yemen
Islamic Zakat Society	Palestine
ISRC (Islamic Relief Committee)	Sri Lanka
ISWA (Islamic Welfare Association)	Lebanon
Karama Organisation for Women & Children Development	Palestine
LARA	Mozambique

Makassed Islamic Charitable Hospital	Palestine
Mandwi	Nepal
MAP (Medical Aid for Palestinians)	Palestine
Médecins Du Monde (MDM)	Yemen/Palestine
Medrar Foundation	Lebanon
Moroccan Children's Trust	Morocco
Mother Help Age	Kashmir (India)/ UK
Muslim Aid	Bangladesh
Muslim Charity	Pakistan / Bangladesh / Malawi/ Myanmar/ Nepal/ Somalia
Muslim Hands	Afghanistan/ Rwanda
Myittar Resource Foundation	Myanmar
NDEO (Nabd for Development & Evolution)	Yemen
Novo Jibon	Bangladesh/ UK
ORCD (Organisation for Research and Community Development)	Afghanistan
Organisation for Help Out (OHO)	Ethiopia
Orphans In Need	India
Palestinian Farmers' Union	Palestine
PAWS	Pakistan
Penny Appeal Australia	New Zealand
Penny Appeal Bangladesh	Bangladesh
Penny Appeal Gambia	Gambia/ Nigeria
Penny Appeal Israel/Palestine	Palestine
Penny Appeal Nepal	Nepal
Penny Appeal Pakistan	Pakistan
Penny Appeal South Africa	South Africa/ Zimbabwe/ Swaziland/ Malawi/ Lesotho
PEP (Poverty Eradication Program)	Bangladesh
PKPU Human Initiative	Indonesia/ Myanmar

RDC Nepal (Rural Development Centre)	Nepal
RDD (Responsiveness for Relief and Development)	Yemen
READ Foundation	Pakistan/Kashmir
RISDA	Bangladesh
Rumah Zakat	Indonesia/ Myanmar
Rural Aid	Pakistan
Saba Relief	Yemen
SAJIDA Foundation	Bangladesh
SAWA For Development and Aid	Lebanon
Sawaed Assocation	Palestine
Shushilan	Bangladesh
SJA (Sylhet Jubo Academy)	Bangladesh
SMKK	Bangladesh
SOS Children's Villages	Palestine
Syria Relief	Syria / Turkey / Iraq (North)
Taawon	Palestine
Tamar Institute	Palestine
Tamdeen Youth Foundation	Yemen
The Humanitarian Forum Yemen	Yemen
The World Federation	Kenya/ Tanzania/ Pakistan/Iraq
TLC (The Leadership College)	South Africa
TPO (Transcultural Psychosocial Organisation)	Uganda
United Purpose	Senegal/ Malawi/ Bangladesh/ Mozambique / Brazil/ Rwanda
UNRWA	Palestine
UOSSM (Union of Medical Care and Relief Organizations)	Turkey
UST (Unnayan Shahojogy Team)	Bangladesh
Watan Foundation	Syria/ Turkey
Yardimeli	Turkey

Zakat Al Quds	Palestine
Zamzam Charitable Trust	Bangladesh

United Kingdom

UK Partnerships
Adult Psychological Therapy Services Fieldhead
Advance Minerva
Afghan Association
Age UK Bradford
Al-Manaar
Anesis Church
Ashcroft Care Home
Asian Resource Foundation Nepal
Baroness Warsi Foundation
Blue Triangle
Barnado's
Brentwood Hall Care
British Asian Trust
British Red Cross
Burnley Boys and Girls club
Carlisle Council
Clements Gate
CMA Welfare Trust
Common Purpose
Convert Care Programme
Cozy Sleep
Department for Communities and Local Government
Department for International Development/Foreign, Commonwealth & Development Office
Ealing Recovery Team

Ealing Victim Support

East London Mosque

Eden Girls School

EEE Council

Elmbridge Council

Faith in Leadership (SFLP)

Family Lives

FODIP (Forum for Discussion of Israel & Palestine)

Global Human

Great Ormond Street Hospital

Greenford Locality Team

Greystone Community Centre

Grimes Dyke Primary School

Haji Cash and Carry

Happy Days UK Homeless Charity

Hestia Anti-Trafficking Team

Hestia (Ealing)

Highgate Beds

Home Start Hounslow Domestic Violence Outreach Services

Housing for Women

Human Charity Foundation

Initial Accommodation Centre (Urban House) Wakefield

Intensive Support Team

Islamia Schools Trust

Islamic Society of Britain

Khidmat Centre

LaunchGood

Leeds Childrens Heart Hospital

Leeds Teaching Hospital

Lido Centre

MACFEST

MADE

Manchester Foundation Trust Charity

Manchester Royal Infirmary Hospital

Maria House Refuge

Markfield Institute of Higher Education

Martin House Hospice

Meeting Point Leeds

Metropolitan Police

Mother & Child Domestic Violence

Muhammade Welfare Foundation

Mullaco Ltd

Muslim Council of Britain

Muslim Youth Helpline

My Lahore

Nida

Northold Locality Team

Outward Bound

Patching Lodge Hanover

PricewaterhouseCoopers

Rawdat Wamadares Noor Al Salam

Red Bag

Riverside Care and Support

Roti Junction

Royal London Hospital

Sadaqa Day

SAFE Ealing Children's Services

Seafresh

Seekers Hub

Shade 7 Limited Publishing

Shakti

Slough Islamic Schools Project

Spirit of 1873 Ltd

St Basil's

St Catherine's Church

Sufra NW London

Sunrise Catering

Surrey Council

The All-Party Parliamentary Group (APPG) on British Muslims

The Ark Glasgow

The Food & Support Drop-In Halifax

The Global Muslim Film Festival

The Maqam Centre

The Omar Regan Foundation

The Scout Association

Ulfa Aid – Rumi's Cave

University College London Hospital

Victim Support

Viral Kindness Scotland

Wakefield Council

Wakefield District Domestic Abuse Service

Wakefield District Housing

Wakefield Hospice

Well Women Centre

Wellsprings Nursing Home

West Yorkshire Police

Yusuf/Cat Stevens

Yusuf Islam Foundation

Appendix Two: Penny Appeal Programmes

100% Zakat
Adopt A Gran
Aqiqa
Coronavirus Emergency
East Africa Flood
Education First
Emergency Response
Feed Our World
Fidya/Kaffarah
Fitrana
Forgotten Children
Fragile Lives

Gaza Emergency
Hifz Orphan
Indonesia Emergency
Lebanon Emergency
Muharram
Open Your Eyes
OrphanKind
Penny Appeal at Home
Qurbani
Rohinyga Emergency
Sadaqah / Give Sadaqah
Sadaqah Jariyah

Say I Do
Support Our Work
Syria Emegency
The Mosque Project
The Phoenix Fund
Thirst Relief
Uyghur Emergency
Waqf
Winter Emergency
Women's Welfare
Yemen Crisis

Appendix Three: The People

They say people come into your life for a reason, a season, or a lifetime. I'm forever grateful for the unique ways each of these individuals have touched my life and the life of Penny Appeal. There are too many to mention, but I'll try my best.

Abby Ghafoor
Abdelmuti Tirawi
Abdul Varachhia
Abdullah Bustami
Abrar Hussain
Aina Khan
Akmal Saleem
Ali Khan
Amir Hussain
Anil Mussarat
Anne-Marie Huby
Arberor Hadri
Arshad Ashraf
Asghar Ali
Asif Rangoonwala
Asif Sadiq MBE
Atifa Shah
Azhar Qayuma
Azim Kidwai
Bara Kherigi
Barrister Kaiser Nazir
Baron Bilimoria CBE
Baron Bourne of

Aberystwyth
Baroness Sayeeda Warsi
Baroness Uddin
Bilal Gahfoor
Boonaa Mohammed
Bushra Sheikh
Chris Blauvelt
David Holmes
DCC Mabs Hussain MBE
Denise Jeffery
Dr Abdul Bari
Dr Amjad Parvez
Dr Hina Shahid
Dr Ikram Butt
Dr Imran Hakim
Dr Kotecha
Dr Nighat Awan OBE
Dr Rosena Allin Khan MP
Dr Husna Ahmad OBE
Dr Zahid Parvez
Ed Prior
Faisal Ali
Faryal Makhdoom Khan
Farzana & Jules Rahman
Fatima Patel
Furqan Naeem
Golam Rasul
Hafiz Mughal
Haider Choudrey
Hamid Azad
Harris Bokhari OBE
Harun Rashid Khan
Hassan Joudi
Hassen Rasool

Hayyan Ayaz
Hinduja Brothers
Hitan Mehta
Iain McNicol
Ian Winterbottom
Ifti Ifrahim
Iftikhar Azam
Imam Abdullah Hasan
Iqbal Nasim MBE
Irfan Bostan
Ishfaq Farooq
Ismail Murad
Javed Huq
Javed Hussain
Jehangir Malik OBE
Jonaed Afzal
Jordon Warburton
Julie Siddiqui
Junaid Afzal
Kadeer Arif
Kalim Aslam
Kashif Shabir
Kevin Tricket
Khalid Isaacs
Khalid Raza
Lady Ghazala Hamid
Luqman Ali
Malik Chaudhary
Malik Khan
Mamoon Yusaf
Mary Creagh
Mike Denby
Miqdad Versi
Mohamed Ali

Mohammed Amersi
Muddassar Ahmed
Mustafa Field
Dr Myriam Francois
Na'ima Roberts
Nadeem Javaid MBE
Naeem Sattar
Nahida Kayum
Nasir Sharif
Nassar Hussain
Natasha Syed
Naveed Asghar
Navinder Grover
Naz Shah MP
Nazia Khatun
Nizam Uddin OBE
Nusrat Bashir
Nyla Jan
Oli Barrett
Omar Shahid
Onjali Rauf
Othman Moqbel
Peter Box
Peter Roberts
Qari Asim MBE
Quabir Hussain
Rabia Bhatti
Remona Aly
Richard Donner
Riz Ahmed
Rizwan Malik
Rooful Ali
Roohi Hasan
Saad Awan
Sadiq Khan – Mayor of London
Sajjad Hussain
Saker Nusseibeh CBE
Salim Kassam
Sam Wright
Saqib Naseer
Sarah Joseph OBE
Sarfaraz Manzoor
Shabir Patel
Shabir Randeree CBE
Shahid Azeem
Shahid Sheikh OBE
Shakoor Ahmed
Sharif Hassan Al Banna
Sheikh Madani
Shelina Janmohamed
Shuaib Khan
Sir Anwar Pervez

Sir Rodney Walker
Steve Roper
Steven Lewis
Sufyan Ismail
Tabassum Awan
Tariq Shah
Tariq Usmani MBE
The Lord Charles St Oswald DL
Tina Turner
Tom Kaye
Tom Stannard
Tremayne Ducker
Tufail Hussain
Usman Ali
Uzair Bawany
Wakkas Khan
Waleed Jahangir
Wali-Ur-Rahman
Wasim Khalfey
Younis Choudhry
Zaheem Aksar
Zameer Choudrey
Zara Sultana MP
Zohra Khaku
Zulfi Karim
Zumi Farooq

The 2021 Global Penny Appeal Family

These are the heroes that have poured their energies into building Penny Appeal bigger and better than I could ever imagine it to be.

UK & MIDDLE EAST
CEO : Harris Iqbal (UK)
CEO : Mohamed Bali (Middle East)
BOARD:
Isha Begum
Mohammed Jahangir
Rizwan Khaliq
Umber Farooque Sheraz

USA
CEO : Oussama Mezoui
BOARD:
Ahmed Abdel-Saheb
Naiel Iqbal
Safaa Ibrahim
Shaun Ahmed

AUSTRALIA
CEO : Mohamed Mayat
BOARD:
Dr Muhammad Khan
Saif Ahmad
Soad Mehana

SOUTH AFRICA
CEO : Shahnaaz Paruk
BOARD:
Ahmad Abdul
Latiff Mponda
Naseema Mall
Nazeer Jamal

CANADA
CEO : Talha Ahmed
BOARD:
Aleem Hussain
Ramz Aziz

The Organisations
Great people build great institutions. I'm grateful to have interacted with, learnt from and often collaborate with a whole host of organisations, and they all deserve a special mention:

10 Downing Street
Al-Buruj Press
Al-Rayan Bank
Awakening Music
Aziz Foundation
BCBN
Bradford Council for Mosques
British Asian Trust
Buckingham Palace
Chaiiwala
Charity Commission
Chickanos
Convey
Council for Hajj
DEC
Desi Dolls
DfID / FCDO
East London Mosque
Emerald Network
Faith Forum for London
Fundraising Regulator

Hadith of the Day
Highgate Beds
Islam Channel
Islam21C
Islamic Foundation
Islamic Relief
Islamic Society of Britain
JustGiving
LaunchGood
Leeds Makkah Masjid
London Marathon
MB Trading House
MEND
Ministry of Housing,
Community and Local
Government
Mosaic
Muntada Aid
Muslim Aid
Muslim Association of
Britain
Muslim Charities Forum
Muslim Council of Britain
Muslim Doctors
Association
Muslim Influencer Network
MyLahore
National Zakat Foundation
Oxfam
Pure Gym
Regal Foods
Riders of Shaam
SeaFresh
Shahid Afridi Foundation
Signature Trading
The All-Party Parliamentary
Group on British Muslims
The ARK (Glasgow)
The Concordia Forum
Tour De Hajj
Wahed Invest
Wakefield Council
Wakefield Hospice
Wakefield One
World Federation
Yeme Architects
Yielders
Zakat Doctor

The Media
Often misunderstood, we
owe a lot to our media

outlets who perform an
incredible public service.
I'm grateful to have had a
relationship with so many
media professionals, these
are just some of the outlets
that hold a special place in
my heart.

Al Jazeera
Asian Express
Asian Image
Asian Leader
Asian Today
Asian World
BBC
BBC Asian Network
British Muslim TV
Christan Today
Daily Mirror
Dawn Pakistan
Eman Channel
Evening Standard
Fundraising Magazine
GEO News
Huffpost
ITV
MSN News
Ramadan TV
SKY
Sunday Asian Times
The Independent
The Metro
The Muslim Vibe
The New York Times
The Telegraph & Argus
Third Sector
TopicUK Magazine
TRT
TV One
Unity FM
Wakefield Express
Wakefield First
Yorkshire Post
5Pillars

The Award Bodies
It's a deep honour to be
recognised by industry
leaders for the work
you've done. I'm grateful
in particular for these

awarding bodies who have
sung our praises far and
wide:

Asian Achievement Awards
Asian Media Awards
Awards and Accolades:
Bond International
Development Awards
British Muslim Awards
English Asian Awards
IOD Director of the Year
JustGiving Awards
Muslim 100
Muslim Charities Forum
Nachural Entrepreneurship
Awards
Natwest Entrepreneur for
Good Awards
Prime Minister's Points of
Light Award
The Digital Awards
Third Sector Excellence
Award
Wakefield Express Awards
Yorkshire Choice Awards

The Scholars
Our spiritual mentors and
guides are the ones who
inspire us to be the change
that we want to see in the
world. I'm grateful for the
wisdom and foresight each
of these teachers have
imparted that has helped
us along our way:

Abdur Raheem Green
Abdur-Raheem McCarthy
Dr Musharaf Hussein
Imam Siraaj Wahaj
Mufti Yusuf Akudi
Sheikh Abdullah Hakim
Quick
Sheikh Ajmal Masroor
Sheikh Amer Jamil
Sheikh Atabek Shukurov
Sheikh Babikir Ahmed
Babikir
Sheikh Hisham Mahmoud
Sheikh Abdalhaqq Bewley

Sheikh Idriss Watts
Sheikh Ibrahim Mogra
Sheikh Navaid Aziz
Sheikh Redha Bedeir
Sheikh Yusuf Estes
Usama Canon
Yusuf Chambers

**And a special mention
to the scholars who
were featured in the
Penny Appeal sponsored
Reviving of the Islamic
Spirit UK:**
Dr Umar Farooq Abdullah
Imam Zaid Shakir
Sheikh Muhammad bin
Yahya an-Ninowy
Sheikh Yahya Rhodus
Yusuf Islam

The Former Trustees
Since our inception our
board has evolved quite
a bit, but one thing that
has stayed the same is the
talent and zeal that our
board members boast.
Special thanks to those
who have been there from
the beginning:

Dr Shama Firdous
Eric Timmins
Ian Wainwright
Jo Marshall
Sofina Ilyas (Late)

**The Former Staff and
Contractors**
The dream works because
our teams work! These
individuals have each
poured blood, sweat
and tears into building a
movement to serve those
most vulnerable at home
and abroad. From the
bottom of my heart,
thank you.

Aamer Naeem OBE
Abdul Aziz
Abdul Raheem Aksar
Abdul Sammad Aftab
Abdul Wahab
Adnan Hussain
Aferdita Pacrami
Ahtsham Yousaf
Akif Ehsan
Akif Raja
Amy Jackson
Arslan Moghal
Asim Rahman
Asim Satar
Barrister Rizwan Hussain
Basharat Alam
Basharat Hussain (Late)
Dr Hanif Malik OBE
Ebrahim Khamissa
Ejaz Ali
Fozia Shah
Gemma Rathbone
Gill Laidler
Gulam Younis
Haroon Kala
Hasen Mahmood
Hassnain Haider
Hayden Kurek
Hazel Normandale
Ilyas Salim
Keisha Knights
Khalil Benkhalil
Kubra Hussain
Laura Siragher
Majed Saqr
Majid Hussain
Mansha Fazel
Mohammad Quadan
Mohammad Sajid Sarwar
Mohammed Imran
Mohammed Naji
Nabila Saddique
Nadeem Tahir
Nadia Rasul
Nailah Naeem
Nazakath Khan
Numaan Shahid
Pasha Shah
Pedro Carvalho
Qadeer Qureshi
Qari M Bilal

Razwan Faraz
Ridwana Wallace-Laher
Samia Hussain
Sarah Joseph OBE
Shabana Ali
Shafi Khan
Shahfaaz Saeed
Sibbat E-Noor
Sonia Mitchell
Taf Mohammed
Tariq Jahan
Tay Jiva MBE
Umran Amin
Wasim Akhtar
Yaseen Sheikh
Yasmin Elhady
Yasmin Gill
Youssef Farhat
Zaheer Khan
Zahid Rahman
Zahida Kayum
Zain Luqman Miah
Zarafshaan Hussain

The Presenters
It's one thing to have a
dream, it's another entirely
to be able to inspire tens of
thousands to dream with
you. This is what these
talented individuals did for
us and I'm grateful to each
of you

Abdullah Afzal
Abdullah Hakim Quick
Abdullah Haqqani
Ahmed Bostan
Ajmal Masroor
Alyas Karmani
Atif Iqbal
Bilal Hassam
Dean Nusrat
Faraz Yousafzai
Guz Khan
Habib Malik
Ibrahim Mogra
Imran Safdar
Na'eem Raza
Navaid Aziz
Rahim Jung

Reda Bedeir
Samina Ahmed
Suhail Ahmed-Qadri
Usman Rehman

The Ambassadors, past and present
These individuals have accomplished so much in their lives for them to lend their support to Penny Appeal means the world to me and more.

Amir Khan
Dr Hany El Banna OBE
Ebrahim Rasool
James Caan CBE
Lady Barbara Judge CBE (Late)
Mehwish Hayat TI
Safe Adam
Yusuf / Cat Stevens

The Comedians
Comedy is a funny way of being serious and these guys have done just that, championing critical conversations, inspiring us to reflect while all the while cracking us up at the same time!

Azeem Muhammad
Azhar Usman
Fatiha El-Ghorri
Jeff Mirza
Kae Kurd
Mo Amer
Moses The Comic
Nabil Abdulrashid
Omar Hamdi
Omar Regan
Paul Chowdhury
Preacher Moss
Prince Abdi
Ramy Youssef
Tez Ilyas

Not forgetting...
The names too awesome to fit into just one category but still deserve a mention nonetheless! Allah bless each of you with the best in this life and the next. Ameen.

Aatif Nawaz
Alman Nusrat
Harris J
Iman Farrar
Isam Bachiri
Maher Zain
Mista Islah
Nader Khan
Pearls of Islam
Rashid Khan
Sami Yusuf
Shakira, AKA Kid Boss
The Panto family
Waqas Qadri

Appendix Four: Rationale for this Book

In 2020, the trustees of Penny Appeal approved the decision to publish *Small Change, Big Difference: The Story of Penny Appeal* to coincide with the beginning of Ramadan in 2021 (12 April). Working with an experienced and successful British publishing company, we established a budget that would allow us to produce a commercial-quality book that can be sold in physical and online bookshops as a means of raising funds for the charity. All revenue after publishing costs have been covered will go directly to Penny Appeal. Our intention is for the book to remain available for sale around the world for at least a few years. Every purchase of this book, therefore, benefits the charity, and I would like to thank you, reader, for your contribution.

With thanks

The publisher would like to thank the following for their contributions to the making of this book: Simon Petherick, Waseem Mahmood, Mitchell Albert and Shannon Clinton-Copeland for their editorial guidance. James Shannon, Arberor Hadri and Wasim Khalfey for design and typesetting. Irfan Bostan for team managing and all the Penny Appeal team around the world. And of course, Adeem Younis, for the inspiration and strength to tell this story. And finally, a word of thanks for all not mentioned here for the small changes, they have made a big difference. Please do consider using the donation envelope enclosed in the back of this book to support the great work of Penny Appeal around the world.

Thank you.

Adeem Younis is a multi-award winning, Yorkshire-born entrepreneur and philanthropist.

Adeem Younis founded his first business, www.SingleMuslim.com, aged 17 above a pizza shop he worked for in Wakefield. What started as a leap into the unknown, grew into the world's largest Muslim matrimonial service, reaching over a million members in the UK and a further three million around the world.

Not content with this entrepreneurial success, Adeem fused his winning digital skills with his desire and passion to help those less fortunate in life than himself. In 2009, he founded Penny Appeal – an award-winning and Guinness World Record-holding humanitarian charity. His inspired vision, daring strategies and tremendous work ethic have enabled Penny Appeal to raise over £100 million for good causes across the world. The success and impact of both the charity and www.SingleMuslim.com have thrust Adeem into a senior leadership role in the British Muslim community and beyond.

He was appointed an Ambassador of The Yorkshire Society seeking to improve cohesion amongst divided communities. He was decorated as the 2017 'NatWest Great British Entrepreneur for Good' and in the same year received a Highly Commended National Award by the Institute of Directors. He also won Entrepreneur of the Year in Wakefield Business Awards 2018 and won Charity Chair of the Year at the 2018 Third Sector Excellence Awards. And in 2019, he received the Prime Minister's Points of Light award for outstanding individuals making a change in their community.